pathways to power

by Merrill F. Unger

Author of
"Introductory Guide to
the Old Testament"

ZONDERVAN PUBLISHING HOUSE
GRAND RAPIDS, MICHIGAN

Printed in the United States of America

17358

CONTENTS

FOREWORD

The devotional essays which appear in the present volume consist of a selection from the articles of the author which have appeared in various Christian periodicals during the last five years. Thanks is expressed to *The Evangelical Christian, Moody Monthly, Eternity, The King's Business, Christian Victory (Grace and Truth)* and *The Alliance Weekly* for permission to use those articles which from time to time appeared in their pages.

The author sends forth this devotional collection with an earnest prayer that it will be an inspiration to God's people to press on in those paths that lead to spiritual power and deeper fellowship with our Lord and Saviour Jesus Christ.

CHAPTER ONE

THE PATHWAY OF PRAYER

But we have this treasure in earthen vessels, that the excellency of the power may be of God, and not of us.

II CORINTHIANS 4:7

Keeping the Morning Watch

My voice shalt Thou hear in the morning, O Lord, in the morning will I direct my prayer unto Thee, and will look up (Psalm 5:3).

A CHRISTIAN should start every new day with God. He should never meet others until he has first met God alone in the inner chamber of prayer. This early morning meeting with God we shall call "The Morning Watch" or the devotional hour, the time when we talk with God and God talks with us. We should give this time to God because it is the time when we are rested and refreshed as a result of a night's slumber. It is the time when our physical, mental and spiritual powers are at their very best. The time when we are most able to think clearly and seek God's presence most ardently. And since God deserves the very best we can give, He deserves this morning hour, the best hour of our day.

The pious heart of David, a "man after God's own heart," was thinking and pondering over the morning watch when in holy worship he cried out to God, "My voice shalt Thou hear in the morning, O Lord, in the morning I will direct my prayer unto Thee, and will look up." It was this morning by morning meeting with God, this intimate and holy communion with Jehovah, that made David a man after God's own heart. Let us faithfully keep the morning devotional throughout the years and we, too, like David, shall become men and women after God's own heart.

No one can be much in another's presence without becoming like that one. "Show me your company and I will

7

tell you what you are," is true also with God. You spend much time in His presence, and you will become like Him. Can you not see David, the shepherd lad, out there on the Judaean hillsides feeding the sheep? The first faint streaks of dawn on the eastern sky find the shepherd lad on his knees before God. And as the newly-risen sun gilds the dew-bedecked grass and flowers, David is still on his knees talking to God, and God is talking to him. As the rays of the sun stream down upon the earth, so the beams of God's love and grace flood David's soul, and give him strength and grace to meet the lion and the bear in single-handed conquest. If David needed to give God these early hours of every day, naturally large-hearted and magnanimous as he was, how much more need we, narrow, mean and selfish as we frequently are.

Often as we study the life of that greater than David, David's Lord, we find Him keeping the morning watch. The dawn of a new day always found Jesus in earnest prayer to His Heavenly Father. Alone on the mountain, yea, a great while before daybreak we find Him in holy rapt communion with the Father. Often we discover Him spending whole nights in prayer before God. If Jesus needed to keep the morning watch and needed to get alone with the Father for strength and grace for each day — He the pure, sinless, spotless Son of God that He was, how much more do we, who are encompassed with sin, and surrounded with infirmity! Most of us little realize the great importance and necessity of keeping the morning watch.

A day cannot be started properly if it is not started with God. Failure will be the consequence unless we call upon God at the beginning of every day. This meeting with God is so important and indispensable that we ought never to let anything or anyone come between us and God to rob us of its observance. Realizing, then, the far-reaching importance of this time alone with God in the early morning, let us examine a few suggestions which will aid us in its observance.

Andrew Murray, that mighty man of God who was so familiar with the deep things of God, says, "It is in the closet, in the morning watch, that our spiritual life is both tested and strengthened. There is the battlefield where it is to be decided every day whether God is to have all, whether our life is to be absolute obedience. If we can conquer there, the victory during the day is sure."

I. LOVE FOR OUR LORD SHOULD BE THE MOTIVATING PRINCIPLE WHICH PROMPTS OUR OBSERVANCE OF THE MORNING WATCH

1. *Shall We Regard It As Simply a Duty?* It is such, and a necessary part of our religious life, but if we observe it merely because we consider it a duty, it will soon become a heavy burden. It will then be a mere routine piece of business, like a job, which we have, not because we like it, but because it means our livelihood. Never must the morning hour with God be reduced to the level of work, or an unpleasant duty, which somehow must be performed because we count ourselves Christians, and we know that Christians are supposed to pray.

2. *Shall We Consider Our Own Happiness and Well-Being the Compelling Motive?* If our own welfare is the chief thought, that will not supply the motive power to make it successful and attractive. Of course, faithful and sustained observance of this hour will assure joy and spiritual well-being, but never will these motives furnish a sufficient stimulus for keeping it.

3. *Let Our Desire for Fellowship with God Be the All-Compelling Motive.* This and this alone will suffice to make the morning hour fresh and inviting. To have a desire for God — to know Him better, experience His love, receive from His loving heart grace and strength, to have our lives filled with His presence — this is the purpose that should make

us enter the inner chamber, shut the door, and be alone with God as we start every new day. "This is the day which the Lord hath made; we will rejoice and be glad in it" (Psalm 118:24).

The morning watch should be love's trysting place. It should be the place where we meet our dearest and best Friend. For that is what Jesus is and should be to each of us. Whoever heard of the meeting of two good friends being dull and tedious. If, however, you must daily meet one for whom you care little, the meetings soon become unpleasant, the sooner over the better. That is why the so-called "sweet hour of prayer" is any thing but sweet to so many professing Christians. A genuine love for the Lord must be the heart impulse leading us to keep the devotional hour, alone with God.

II. There Should Be a Definite Place for the Observance of the Morning Watch

1. *Every Christian Should Have Some Designated Place for Prayer.* There should be some secret spot, some solitary nook where he can be alone with God. Jesus, our great Teacher of prayer, gives this as one of His first lessons. "But thou, when thou prayest, enter into thine inner chamber, and having shut the door, pray to thy Father in secret, and thy Father which seeth in secret shall recompense thee openly" (Matthew 6:6). This "inner chamber" is the school-room, where Jesus teaches His lessons in prayer.

It is not that worship is confined to any one place or time. Jesus emphatically taught otherwise in His words to the Samaritan woman. True prayer must be in spirit and truth. Yet our Lord wants us to have a definite spot where we can daily meet Him. That spot may be anywhere. It may change from day to day, if we change our abode. But we must have that quiet, secluded place, where we can enter the Master's presence. It may be beside our bed, or a nook in the attic. It must be somewhere away from the noise of human voice and human bustle.

2. *Why Is This Secret Place of Prayer So Essential?* Our Father, the great and loving God whom we meet, is Himself in secret. He is the concealed One, the invisible One. He does not manifest Himself to unsanctified eyes, nor reveal Himself to uncircumcised ears. He is the infinitely holy God, and hence hidden from sinners. Communion with Him is the most valuable treasure a man can possess. It is more valuable than precious gems. Like treasures on this earth, like a rich vein of gold ore, or some great and splendid diamond, it lies hidden. There is a secret to finding the treasure. The secret is in the secret place of prayer.

Our Father, who is in secret, will not lift the veil from His presence as long as we are occupied with our own thoughts, desires and ambitions. To meet Him we must enter the closet and shut the door. This shutting the door speaks symbolically of shutting out every worldly voice, every worldly desire, and motive, and shutting ourselves in with God alone! Only then will His gracious presence be revealed to us and His almighty power made operative in us. This is the secret of meeting God.

Remember He is in secret and reveals Himself in the secret place. Do you, like multitudes of Christians, complain that your prayer life is not what it ought to be? You feel so weak and helpless and sinful in prayer? Go into the inner chamber, close the door, and remember the loving Heavenly Father waits to meet and bless you there.

3. *What Is the Reward of the Secret Place?* "And thy Father which seeth thee in secret shall reward thee openly" (Matthew 6:6). Here Jesus assures us that secret prayer can never be fruitless. It is bound to be rewarded with blessing in our life, openly, before the eyes of men. You meet God in private, and He will bless you in public, before the eyes of the multitude. "He that cometh to God must believe that

He is and that He is a rewarder of them that diligently seek Him" (Hebrews 11:6). Your reward for prevailing prayer will be power with God and with men (Genesis 32:28).

III. THE READING OF THE WORD OF GOD SHOULD BE A VITAL PART OF THE MORNING WATCH

1. *The Bible Plays a Very Important Part In Our Devotions, and Is Meant To Point Us to God, But Unless We Are Very Careful, the Word May Actually Intervene and Hide Him from Us.* So many good Christians are led astray here. As they read the Word in the morning watch, the mind becomes so enraptured and delighted with what it finds there, that the whole reading of the Bible becomes a matter of the head rather than the heart. Little spiritual good is thus accomplished. If our reading of the Word does not minister to the refining of our lives, it becomes a hindrance rather than a help.

How many children of God there are, who are real students of the Word, and yet who are deficient in the most elementary graces of the Christian life. How many are proud of their Biblical knowledge. "Knowledge puffeth up, but love buildeth up" (I Corinthians 8:1). How many are sectarian, narrow, argumentative and contentious, because they read the Word, perchance know its letter well, but rarely meditate upon it devotionally, so that it feeds the soul, and ministers to a consistent growth in grace. How often, too, are there Bible teachers who can give clear expositions of the Word, but whose teaching is characterized by frigidity. Whereas some simple unlearned evangelist in touch with God can warm and melt our hearts as he recounts the simple story of the cross.

2. *It Is a Good Practice in Our Morning Watch to Cultivate the Habit of Reading the Word of God Humbly.* There must be a sincere dependence upon the Spirit of God to teach us. We must always realize that the Word of God can only be comprehended and appropriated as the Holy Spirit takes it

and administers it to our hearts. No matter how brilliant you
may be intellectually, or what educational advantages you may
have had, simple child-like dependence upon the Spirit is all-
essential, if you would understand the most elementary prin-
ciples of the Kingdom of God.

Never must we read the Word in our devotional hours
with the aim of merely gaining Biblical facts and knowledge.
We must read it to get the power of it into our lives. If we
read the Word merely to get intellectual knowledge, it will
not change our hearts any more than reading a popular novel.
Any man who would enter the hidden mysteries and deep
riches of the Word must ever approach it very humbly, and
in simple and child-like dependence on the Spirit of God.

3. *Our Reading of the Word of God Should Ever Be in
an Attitude of Unreserved Surrender to the Will of God As
Revealed By the Word.* It is easy to hear and not do. It is
difficult to live up to the light we receive. It is a dangerous
practice to read the Word of God without a definite and
earnest purpose to obey. It makes us callous and hardens us in
our disobedience. Light received and rejected brings greater
darkness. God's Book is a lamp unto our feet and a light unto
our pathway. It is a terrible sin to have the light shine and
the lamp burn showing us the way and then to refuse to walk
in that way. Let us read the Book of God in our devotions
with sincere and keen desire to put its precepts into immediate
practice.

We should regard the Bible as a chart for guiding us in
the day ahead. Yet, although we must not seek for mere in-
formation or facts in our devotional reading, nevertheless, our
reading can and should be systematic. It is perfectly proper
and desirable to read a whole book through, or even a series of
books, or the whole Bible, book by book.

IV. THERE MUST BE ACTUAL COMMUNION WITH GOD IN THE MORNING WORSHIP

1. *We Must Aim to Contact God.* This is the purpose of all real prayer — to see the face of God, to know and feel He is looking on us, listening to us, and working in us. It is this meeting God that purifies, strengthens and uplifts. Any other kind of prayer is mere repetition of religious words. The joylessness, feebleness and emptiness of our religious life come from our failure to get in contact with God in our prayer time.

Touching God is like touching a live wire. He sends power through our whole being. Any one can touch a dead wire and never be different, or never know that he touched it. No one, however, can touch God and be unmoved. We cry as Isaiah of old "Woe is me for I am undone, for mine eyes have seen Jehovah of Hosts." To meet God thus in our morning watch assures us a day of gracious ministry for others. We need more of God in our lives, more of His purity, more of His love, more of His grace, more of His strength. If all our spiritual help and resources lie in Him, if He is the source and fountain of all blessing and benediction, then our first and foremost care ought to be to meet Him alone in the morning hour.

2. *We Must Make the Renewal of Our Surrender to Absolute Obedience for That Day to Be a Chief Part of the Morning Sacrifice.* Only once can we make a complete surrender, but daily must we renew that consecration. In our morning devotion we should tell God we are His for His perfect will for that day. Ask Him to guide every thought, word, and deed. Confess and forsake any sin or transgression. Let the channel be open. Let the Holy Spirit have right of way. The measure of blessing we receive from the time of prayer will be proportionate to the reality of our consecration.

Considering the dangers that beset our path — the sins, the temptations, the power of the world, the flesh, and the devil — our plea for divine aid and guidance should be most earnest and utterly sincere. To feel the joy of knowing that one is in the center of God's will for the day gives new zest and stamina to our every word and deed. It assures a day when we will have the satisfaction of having by God's grace and help achieved something worthwhile.

How many days can we not all count lost, simply because we failed to keep the morning watch? How often have we found when we thought we were too busy to keep the morning prayer-time, or too busy to keep it properly that we have lost out in the long run? God can bless or withhold His blessing. Luther was so busy one day that he discovered he could not get on without spending three hours in prayer. Often he went to his closet weighed down and well-nigh ready to give up. But after an hour or two of weeping, pleading, prevailing with God he emerged with a glowing light upon his face crying "Vici" . . . "I have conquered!"

3. *We Must Realize That Our Conversation with God Is Not to Be All One-Sided!* Whoever heard in friendly intercourse of one person doing all the talking? There are perhaps a few unpopular people still left who are veritable chatterboxes, and who do not give other folk a chance to get a word in, but they are very ill-bred, uncouth, ignorant and have few, if any friends. They are a bore wherever they go, and refined people are glad to get out of their presence.

It is to be feared that we are sometimes like these unpopular persons in our dealing with God in prayer. We often do all the talking, and do not get quiet long enough for the Lord to speak to us. We need to be still and hear what reply God would give us. What He has to say to us is all-important, and not so much what we have to say to Him. He knows all about us anyway. It is the office of the Holy Spirit to be the voice of God to us. God never speaks until we are quiet before Him.

In the hidden depths of the soul we can have the glowing assurance that we have been heard, that our prayer has been answered, that God has spoken. This is the result of waiting on God, and is the most vital part of our watch, for unless He speaks to us in the depths of our soul there has really been no interchange of thought.

4. *We Must Pray for Others.* This is the highest form of prayer — intercession — when self is forgotten, and we pour out our heart in loving devotion for others. Prayer for personal improvement and joy cannot be prayer of the greatest power. The greatest prayers of the Lord Jesus were for others — for His disciples, for the lost, for His enemies! If we enter upon the morning watch with our best powers and thoughts centered on the needs of others, and dedicate that time to them, we shall soon see what attraction and new interest it will have. God will bless us without our imploring and seeking Him if, in our devotion to others, we forget about our own needs. If there is to be any great increase in the power of God in the church and its work, it will come through the channel of intercessory prayer.

Would that the Spirit of God might impress upon us the importance of this morning watch. On its faithful and successful observance hangs the fate of our Christian life. Are you faithfully keeping this time of prayer? Are you daily in the freshness of each new morning, as the sunlight of a new day streams through the window, beginning the day with God? Or do you jump from your bed at the blare of an alarm clock, hastily say a few words of prayer, hop into your clothes, rush off to the day's work without really having met God and enjoyed the wonderful heaven-sent privilege of communion with Him?

Remember God meant you to start the day with Him. He intended the morning watch to be the very gate of heaven to your soul, through which His power and blessing, like the flooding sunlight, might stream into your being, and from which sacred chamber you might go out to bless others and to walk with Him all the day.

Praying Without Ceasing

> . . . *Men ought always to pray, and not to faint* (Luke
> 18:1). *Pray without ceasing* (I Thessalonians 5:17).

PRAYER is so all-important in every phase of the Christian
life that too much emphasis can scarcely be given it or too
much time or energy devoted to it. It is doubtful that anything permanent or pleasing to God is ever accomplished without it. Through prayer the strongholds of the enemy are
taken, oppositions and obstacles to the progress of the Gospel
are removed, and the power of God released to accomplish the
divine will. Every child of God knows by experience that
prayer moves the hand that made the worlds, and that God
hears the cry of need and distress.

Frequently, however, when requests are denied or de-
layed, faith falters and prayer ceases. It is then that fainting
begins. But fainting is giving up the battle before the victory
is won. And prayer is a battle! It is stopping work before
the harvest is gathered in. And prayer is labor! To faint is
to leave the field of conflict vanquished rather than victor,
when triumph is assured if we but keep on fighting. To faint
is to leave the sheaves standing in the fields to be spoiled by
autumn's rains and winter's blasts, when a few more hours
of toil would assure their being gathered safely into the
barn.

In the light of the ever-present peril confronting the child
of God our Lord most solemnly urges upon His own a double
responsibility—the duty of praying and the corresponding duty
of prevailing in prayer. Likewise the Apostle Paul with the

17

same danger in view presents unceasing prayer to the Thessalonian believers as a divine command.

I. Prayer Is a Duty

It is sad that many people think little of prayer and make less of it. Those who find themselves in such an unhappy state, however, may well question the reality of their salvation. God's people at least keep up an occasional, if not a constant, correspondence with their Heavenly Father. Some consider prayer more as a ritualistic exercise than vital contact with God. Others view it as a comfortable resort in extremity, or as a welcome refuge in distress. To others prayer is a priceless privilege and a heaven-given honor. It is this, of course. But it is more.

1. *Prayer Is an Inescapable Duty.* Comparatively few Christians think of prayer in this light. Yet it is as a duty incumbent upon every believer that Jesus directs our attention to prayer in this passage (Luke 18:1). "Men *ought* to pray!" It is not a question of viewing prayer as an exalted privilege to be cultivated by a few or an ecstatic exercise to be engaged in or not at the believer's choice. Our Lord would have us realize most solemnly that prayer is an obligation resting upon every believer, and that we commit sin if we neglect it.

J. Wilbur Chapman, a widely used evangelist of a past generation, once received a letter from Andrew Murray containing the expression, "the sin of a prayerless life." The evangelist was struck by the thought contained in it, and kept repeating it again and again. "Am I sinning when I do not pray? I hate sin. I am always preaching against it. But is it a sin to be prayerless?" His answer to the question was a widely-blessed sermon entitled, "The Sin of a Prayerless Life."

Sin is usually thought of as a trespass committed or some positive aggressive act. But failing to do what we ought to do is sin just as much as doing what we ought not do. We *ought* to pray. If we do not pray, we commit sin.

Prayerlessness is a sin against God. It is a humbling thought to realize that the infinite heart of the Creator yearns for fellowship with His redeemed creatures. He delighted to walk and talk with our first parents "in the garden in the cool of the day," and undertook to restore the broken communion between Himself and His erring children when they sinned (Genesis 3:8-10). He ever delights to converse with His own, not only in the cool of eventide, but during the heat and burden of the day. His voice may be heard in the weeping that endures for a night as well as in the joy that comes in the morning. We rob Him of His joy when we fail to walk in fellowship with Him.

Prayerlessness is a sin against our fellow man — both the saved and the unsaved. Our prayers are instrumental in the salvation of the lost. Our prayerlessness abandons them to eternal doom. Our intercession for fellow believers is necessary to their edification and progress in spiritual things. Our failure to pray for them accordingly is a defection in our duty toward them and toward God, who has such a vital interest in them as His own. The prophet Samuel had this important truth in mind when he said: "For the Lord will not forsake his people for his great name's sake: because it hath pleased the Lord to make you his people. Moreover, as for me, God forbid that I should sin against the Lord in ceasing to pray for you . . ." (I Samuel 12:22, 23).

Prayerlessness, moreover, is a sin against ourselves. It shuts out the presence and power of God from our lives and robs us of that which is our highest delight and benefit. Prayer is like a refreshing river entering the wilderness and dry land of our hearts, making them "rejoice and blossom as the rose," yea causing them to "blossom abundantly, and rejoice even with joy and singing" (Isaiah 35:1, 2). By prayer "the eyes of the blind" are "opened" and "the ears of the deaf" are "unstopped," "the lame man" is made to "leap as a hart" and the "tongue of the dumb" is made to "sing"

(Isaiah 35:5-6). When we commune with God "the parched ground" becomes "a pool and the thirsty land springs of water" (Isaiah 35:7).

Prayer to the Christian's spiritual life is just as vital as breathing is to his physical life. Taking prayer from a Christian is like depriving a human body of air to breathe.

> Prayer is the Christian's vital breath,
> The Christian's native air;
> His watchword at the gates of death,
> He enters heaven with prayer.

God has put within the reach of all His children the means of being spiritually great and strong. We do not have to be rich, cultured, gifted or intelligent to achieve in the Christian life. We need only to know how to come into God's sacred presence and there in rapt communion and holy worship, obtain all that we need for the highest blessing to ourselves and benefit to others. We may have few talents, but if we learn how to use the talent of prayer, God will make us effective Christians and useful servants.

2. *Prayer Is a Constant Duty.* Not only is prayer an inescapable duty, "men ought . . . to pray," it is also a constant duty, "men ought *always* to pray." The situation could not be otherwise. The word our Lord used is a necessary one. "Men ought *always* to pray" because men *always* need God — not merely upon occasion or in an emergency, as many foolishly imagine, but constantly. Men need God in prosperity as well as adversity, in health as well as in sickness, in joy as well as in sorrow, in strength as well as in weakness. Therefore, men ought always to pray.

So far from men needing God less in times of prosperity than in adversity, they more often need Him more. When "Jeshurun waxed fat . . . then he forsook God, which made him, and lightly esteemed the Rock of his salvation" (Deuteronomy 32:15). It is commonly true when we are weak, we are strong (II Corinthians 12:10), and when we are poorest, we are richest. The unclouded day of prosperity is always fraught with spiritual danger. Pride and self-sufficiency are then most apt to creep in.

In periods of difficulty and seeming defeat temptations no less subtle, but of another sort appear. Unless we persevere in prayer, discouragement lays hold upon us and we faint by the way.

II. PREVAILING PRAYER IS A CORRESPONDING DUTY

Many of God's own who consider prayer an honor and a privilege, and more than that, an inescapable and constant duty, yet have never comprehended the obligation involved to persevere in intercession until the answer is realized or the victory is assured.

1. *Prevailing Prayer Is a Necessity.* It is not sufficient that we pray. It is our duty to "pray through." "Men ought always to pray and *not* to faint." Tremendous opposition of Satan to importunate prayer renders prevailing intercession imperative. There is a vast amount of defeat and wasted energy in prayer because many of God's children quit the battle before the standard of victory is actually hoisted over the enemy's fortress. They leave the field of labor before a finished task brings the reward of rest in the cool of the day. They refuse to drain the full cup of weeping in the night that they might experience the joy that comes in the morning. The enemy stages a victorious comeback before they have driven him from the field, and they are robbed of the trophies of victory.

Prevailing prayer is necessary not only because of Satanic opposition, but also because of God's love for us. Too frequently do we overlook the fact that God delights in our fellowship and would have us in His presence continually. If He always granted us at once the things we desired, we would go away to live in the enjoyment of the gifts and forget the Giver. We would revel in His blessings and lose sight of the Blesser.

But God yearns to give what is incomparably better than His gifts. He desires to give us Himself. Accordingly, He often keeps back the desired blessing in order to draw His waiting child more closely to His infinite heart of love that the trusting one may find delight in Himself alone and say with the poet:

> Once it was the blessing,
>   Now it is the Lord;
> Once it was the feeling,
>   Now it is His Word;
> Once His gift I wanted,
>   Now the Giver own;
> Once I sought for healing,
>   Now Himself alone.
>
> —A. B. *Simpson*

Our gracious Lord seeks to draw us into His presence and into such a place of placid abiding in Him that His answer "No" to our request is just as delightful to us as His answer "Yes." Thus drawn into such experimental oneness with the all-gracious One, there is no room for defeat, despair, or discouragement, nor any place for fainting. "Even the youths shall faint and be weary, and the young men shall utterly fall; but they that wait upon the Lord shall renew their strength; they shall mount up with wings as eagles; they shall run, and not be weary; they shall walk and not faint" (Isaiah 40:30, 31).

2. *Prevailing Prayer Involves Unceasing Prayer.* The Christian's pilgrimage through the world is so beset with dangers, sins and temptations, and the upward way to heaven so harassed by conflicts, foes and difficulties of every description, that unless the believer continually receives supernatural enablement from God through prayer, he will be overcome and cast down into defeat and despair. Realizing this to be true, the apostle issued the injunction to the Thessalonian

saints to "pray without ceasing" (I Thessalonians 5:17). The Apostle Paul issues as a command what our Lord presented as a duty. "Men ought *always* to pray."

But neither our Lord nor Paul, of course, had in mind any thought of men hiding themselves away in a cell of a monastery or withdrawing from other men and spending their lives in selfish isolation apart from the needs of humanity. They did mean, however, that Christians should retire from ministries to men for protracted periods of ministry for men in the secret place of prayer. Certainly Scripture intends that the closest possible tie should exist between prayer and service, making communion and worship in the divine presence the basis of all testimony and ministry to men.

Nor did our Lord and the Apostle Paul mean to convey the impression that to "pray always" and to "pray without ceasing" men have to be constantly in the formal exercise or posture of prayer. In the contrary they would have us understand that prayer is not so much a formal exercise or a particular posture as an attitude of heart and mind. The exercise of unceasing prayer is rather a matter of complete yieldedness and constant dependence upon God. Although no formal words of petition or praise may be uttered at the moment or a formal posture of prayer assumed, with the free flow of the Holy Spirit through the surrendered and obedient life, the believer's every activity and ministry constitutes a prayer. His whole life becomes a savor of sacrifice and praise to God, a delightful unbroken communion with the Father above. Happy are those who find this holy portal. To those who enter, it becomes the gateway to heaven upon earth.

Child of God, have you entered this sacred door of ministry? Is prayer to you merely a delight, or a haven in the time of storm, or only a privilege of which you avail yourself occasionally? Will you not accept it as your inescapable and constant duty? Will you so yield to God that your whole

life may become an unceasing prayer to God and a benediction
to men?

> Lord, what a change within us one short hour
> Spent in Thy presence would prevail to make!
> What heavy burdens from our bosoms take,
> What parched grounds revive as with a shower;
> We kneel, and all around us seems to lower;
> We rise, and all, the distant and the near
> Stands forth a sunny outline brave and clear.
>
> We kneel, how weak! we arise, how full of power!
> Why, therefore, should we do ourselves this wrong,
> Or others, that we are not always strong;
> That we are ever overborne with care;
> That we should ever weak or heartless be,
> Anxious or troubled, when with us is prayer,
> And joy and strength and courage are with Thee?
>
> *—Archbishop Trench*

Defeating Our Spiritual Foes

Put on the whole armour of God, that ye may be able to stand against the wiles of the devil (Ephesians 6:11). *Praying always with all prayer and supplication in the Spirit . . .* (Ephesians 6:18).

THE NECESSITY for unceasing prayer becomes more apparent to the believer as he faces his spiritual foes. Relentlessly active and subtly cunning as they are, the Christian warrior soon discovers that to overcome these spiritual forces arrayed against him he must "pray always with all prayer and supplication in the Spirit . . ." (Ephesians 6:18).

The classic passage describing the inevitable prayer-conflict of the Spirit-filled Christian against the powers of darkness is Ephesians 6:10-20. It is only the Spirit-filled believer, experiencing the power of God in his life, who knows the full meaning of spiritual conflict, for the Spirit-filled experience is the signal for Satanic opposition. God's power in the life *always* stirs up the devil's power of temptation and opposition.

The walk of the Spirit-filled believer is bound to merge into a war as it does in the epistle to the Ephesians. In the first three chapters the apostle outlines the exalted position of the Christian "in the heavenlies in Christ." In the last three chapters he describes the holy walk of the Spirit-filled child of God on earth consonant with his position "in the heavenlies in Christ" (Ephesians 4:1-6:9). Walk inevitably changes into war at chapter 6 verse 10. The Christian pilgrim must become a warrior, and as he walks be prepared to fight.

I. THE WARRIOR'S STRENGTH FOR THE PRAYER CONFLICT IS
HIS POSITION IN CHRIST (verse 10)

The passage begins with that which is of primary importance — strength for the contest. Discussing the source of
this, the apostle reverts to that which is fundamental to the
believer's warfare, as well as his walk; namely, his position
in Christ.

1. *The Christian Is "In Christ."* This organic oneness of
the believer with his Lord is the result of the Spirit's baptizing
ministry placing the child of God in Christ's body, the Church
(I Corinthians 12:13) and into living union with Christ Himself the Head (Romans 6:3, 4). This "in-Christ" position, as
real as the union that exists in the human body between the
various members and the head, is the basis of all the
positions and possessions of the believer.

2. *The Christian's Power in Prayer Springs from His Position in Christ.* "Finally, my brethren, be strong *in the Lord*
. . ." (Ephesians 6:10). The exhortation is not to be strengthened "from the Lord, but that which goes much deeper, "in
the Lord." "Be continually strong" (it is present tense) in
the position which is yours by virtue of your organic union
with Him, just as a hand or foot has its strength from the
body to which it belongs.

It is important to note that the strengthening is such
as can take effect only in union with Christ, and the *strength*
obtained from the exhaustless source is entirely adequate for
triumph in the conflict and is "the *power* of His *might*."
Three different Greek words are necessary to portray the complete efficacy of the divine enablement which is available to
the child of God on the ground of his "in-Christ" position.

Nothing can take the place of the "strength," "power"
and "might" which have their origin in the believer's union
with Christ. Human ingenuity, dynamic personality, and
natural talent or ability are of no avail without it. The

Christian warrior is placed in contact with the inner source of strength before any other resources he may have can help him in the battle against his spiritual antagonists.

Saul's armour was useless against Goliath because the bearer was in wrong relation with the Lord. David could win the battle because he was "strong in the Lord." The clarion call in this hour of appalling need is for Christian warriors who will perceive their strength "in the Lord" and go apart in faith to claim the power of that position and come forth to lead men to victory in the crucial conflicts of the day.

II. The Warrior's Foes in the Prayer Conflict Are Spiritual (verses 11, 12)

The source of the warrior's strength in his union with Christ having been set forth, the apostle proceeds next to identify the believer's enemies. They are his foes, relentless and utterly implacable, because of the position he has "in Christ," and because that vital union is the basis of his triumph over all their malignant subtlety. No more enlightening passage on the person, position, purpose and power of the enemy appears in all the Word of God than this.

1. *The Arch-Enemy and Leader of the Spiritual Host of Evil Is the Devil.* "Put on the whole armour of God, that ye may be able to stand against the wiles of the devil" (Ephesians 6:11). From his fall in the pristine ages of the world's history (Isaiah 14:12-17; Ezekiel 28:12-19) until his temptation of our first parents through the agency of the paradisaical serpent, the malignity of this sinister and majestic creature has been directed against Christ, the Seed of the woman (Genesis 3:15) and the Messianic line to Christ's birth. His fury was loosed against our Lord from the manger in Bethlehem to the Cross on Golgotha's brow.

Today Christ's physical body raised "far above all principality, and power and might and dominion, and every name that is named . . ." (Ephesians 1:21) is beyond Satan's power and malignity. But the risen Son of God is installed in glory as the Head of another body, His Church. This body, still on its earthly pilgrimage, is within Satan's reach. Its identification with Christ, linking it with God's glorious purposes for the eternal future involving Satan's complete overthrow, draws to itself the fierce and subtle attack of the adversary.

Satan does not hesitate to adapt his method of attack to the greatest possible advantage. Failing to accomplish maximum results by violence, fire and sword, he readily resorts to subtlety and every form of deception. So cunning are his stratagems that the wisest warrior could be led astray without God's intervention. The "whole armour of God" is necessary to combat Satan's wiles.

2. *Satan's Helpers Consist of a Vast Highly Organized Army.* "For our wrestling is not against flesh and blood, but against the principalities, against the powers, against the world-rulers of this darkness, against the spiritual hosts of wickedness in the heavenly places" (Ephesians 6:12, R. V.). "The principalities" are commanders-in-chief or five star generals directly under Satan himself. "The powers" are next in rank, serving under the principalities. "The world-rulers of this darkness" are the spiritual potentates that exercise their power through the heads of human governments. "The spiritual hosts of wickedness in the heavenly places" are the least in rank and form the innumerable cohorts of demons who operate upon and through their human agencies.

The Word of God lays great stress on the nature of the conflict. It is emphatically spiritual, being "not against flesh and blood." It is, moreover, "a wrestling," that is, a contest between two in which each endeavors to throw the other. The contest is decided when the victor is able to prostrate his antagonist by holding him down with his hand upon his neck.

The figure could not possibly be more graphic in portray-

ing the seriousness of the struggle. Either the believer defeats his foe or his foe defeats him in a man-to-man encounter
demanding the utmost skill, strength and self-control.

III. THE WARRIOR'S EQUIPMENT FOR THE PRAYER CONFLICT
IS THE ARMOUR OF GOD (verses 13-17)

In the face of such a dread array of highly organized and
inveterately hostile power the Christian warrior might well
feel helpless if not hopeless. But God has anticipated his well-
grounded fears by prefacing the realistic portrayal of his enemy with a heartening account of the Christian's resources of
strength in union with Christ. Lest the believer should still
be overwhelmed by such a sinister hierarchy of celestial
evil drawn up against him, a detailed description of the
effectual equipment God has provided for him is given piece
by piece.

"Wherefore, take unto you the whole armour of God
. . ." (Ephesians 6:13). The encouraging command is "take"
not "make." In the face of such a foe man's attempts to make
his own armour are pitiful indeed. God has made the panoply
in all the perfections of His redemptive grace. All we need
to do is to take it to ourselves "to withstand in the evil day"
when the evil forces advance against us, and "having done all"
in appropriating the strength which is ours in Christ, "to
stand."

1. *The Girdle of Truth and the Breastplate of Righteousness Protect the Body As a Whole.* "Stand therefore, having
your loins girt about with truth, and having on the breastplate
of righteousness" (verse 14). Often beautifully wrought and
gem-studded, the girdle, however, served a more useful purpose than mere ornamentation. It girded the vitals of the
wrestler and the soldier (both figures appear in this passage)
affording the wearer support. Nothing so belts us about
with strength in our warfare against the enemy as the truth
of God's Word.

The breastplate of righteousness shields the most vital regions of the heart, where a wound would more easily prove fatal. To the Thessalonians Paul urged the putting on of "the breastplate of faith and love" (I Thessalonians 5:8), faith being the medium by which we obtain God's righteousness (Rom. 4:5). It is God's righteousness, imputed to us, and ours through faith, that gives us the joyful assurance of our eternal safety in Christ, which no dart of doubt hurled at us by the devil can pierce.

2. *The Gospel of Peace Shields Our Feet.* "And your feet shod with the preparation of the gospel of peace" (verse 15). As the emphasis in this passage is upon standing—". . . that ye may be able to *withstand* in the evil day, and having done all *to stand*" (verse 13), "*stand* therefore" (verse 14)— it is quite essential that the feet be protected. The gospel of God's grace gives the stability we need, because it imparts a peace the world can neither give nor take away, lifting our feet out of the sinking sands of false hopes and placing them upon the solid Rock, Christ Jesus.

3. *The Shield of Faith Equips the Left Hand.* "Above all, taking the shield of faith, wherewith ye shall be able to quench all the fiery darts of the wicked" (verse 16). This item in the equipment is of greater importance than all that has been enjoined because the enemy uses missiles that fly through the air and would prove deadly unless intercepted. Faith is an effective shield to stop these arrows, not only designed to kill, but, being tipped with a burning substance, fashioned to destroy by fire.

4. *The helmet of Salvation Guards the Head.* "And take the helmet of salvation" (verse 17). Experiencing God's salvation in Christ and thereby being indwelt by the Holy Spirit, who guides "into all truth" (John 16:13), the saved man is delivered from the spiritual darkness and skepticism of the natural man (I Corinthians 2:14) and finds his whole range of thinking orientated in spiritual truth.

5. *The Sword of the Spirit Equips the Right Hand.* "And take . . . the sword of the Spirit, which is the word of God" (verse 17). The shield of faith for the left hand to intercept Satan's darts and the sword of the Spirit, the Word of God, for his right hand to cut down the attacking foe! Thus panoplied the warrior may face the enemy victoriously.

IV. THE WARRIOR'S VICTORY IN THE PRAYER CONFLICT IS BY MEANS OF PREVAILING PRAYER (verse 18-20)

Having set forth the Christian warrior's strength and equipment against the enemy, the apostle concludes with an indication of the employment of the Christian's resources.

1. *Prevailing Prayer Is the Christian's Full Employment of His Resources.* "Praying always with *all* prayer and supplication in the Spirit, and watching thereunto with all perseverance and supplication . . ." (verse 18). Prayer in the conflict is not to be construed as "another weapon," as John Bunyan puts it in *Pilgrim's Progress*, asserting that Christian "was forced to put up his sword, and betake himself to another weapon, called All-Prayer . . . " All-prayer is rather the Christian's appropriation of his strength "in the Lord" and his employment of the panoply of God. It comprehends the full gamut of the holy exercise including "supplications, prayers, intercessions, and giving of thanks" (I Timothy 2:1). Above all, it is prayer "in the Spirit" involving spiritual conquest and is no mere repetition of religious words. Accordingly, the devil is routed and the Christian's foes defeated.

2. *Prevailing Prayer Is Unceasing Prayer.* "Praying always . . . with all perseverance . . ." (verse 18). It involves the same elements of constancy and persistency stressed by our Lord when He said, "Men ought *always* to pray and not faint" (Luke 18:1) and by the apostle when he enjoined the Thessalonians to "pray without ceasing" (I Thessalonians 5:17).

3. *Prevailing Prayer Is Expectant Prayer.* It *looks for* an answer. " . . . And watching thereunto with all perseverance

. . ." (verse 18). Prevailing prayer vanquishes the foe and rests in happy contemplation that no frustration can come from the enemy's quarter. On the other hand, it awaits with joyful assurance the revelation of the divine will and power, accepting with equal delight God's "yes" or "no." But God's reply it *must* have, unhindered and unobscured by Satanic interference. Faith reckons this as best and calmly rests in it.

4. *Prevailing Prayer Is Intercessory Prayer.* It rises to the height where self is forgotten and the interests of others are unselfishly taken to heart. "Praying always . . . for *all saints*" (verse 18). "And for me," says the apostle, "that utterance may be given unto me . . ." to "speak boldly, as I ought to speak" (verses 19, 20).

In no period of the world's history have Satanic powers been more blatant and active. Anti-Christian forces are taking over vast sections of the globe. Christianity faces a real threat of extinction. The bugle call is for believers to claim the power that is theirs in union with Christ; to take up the full armour that is theirs through the gracious provision of Christ and to advance victoriously against the enemy on the battlefield of prevailing prayer. It is here that the only real advance can be made. God grant that in this world crisis we may go forward *on our knees.*

> Soldiers of Christ, arise,
>   And put your armour on,
> Strong in the strength which God supplies
>   Through His eternal Son;
> Strong in the Lord of hosts,
>   And in His mighty power,
> Who in the strength of Jesus trusts
>   Is more than conqueror.
>
> Stand then in His great might,
>   With all His strength endued,
> And take, to arm you for the fight,
>   The panoply of God;

That having all things done,
  And all your conflicts past,
  Ye may o'ercome through Christ alone,
  And stand entire at last.

Leave no unguarded place,
  No weakness of the soul;
Take every virtue, every grace,
  And fortify the whole.
From strength to strength go on,
  Wrestle and fight and pray;
Tread all the powers of darkness down,
  And win the well-fought day.

                                    —*Charles Wesley*

Experiencing God's Peace

In nothing be anxious; but in everything by prayer and supplication with thanksgiving let your requests be made known unto God, and the peace of God, which passeth all understanding, shall guard your hearts and your thoughts in Christ Jesus (Philippians 4:6, 7 R. V.).

THERE IS NO BLESSING that brings more positive benefits to the life than the enjoyment of God's peace. While all Christians have experienced peace with God by virtue of exercising saving faith in Christ (Romans 5:1), many of God's children know little of the "peace of God which passeth all understanding" because their lives are not dominated by believing prevailing prayer, which God's Word so closely connects with the enjoyment of His peace.

It is impossible to enjoy God's peace and not face war. The peace is experienced in the midst of war and as a reward for victory in the war, but it can never be experienced *without war*. The reason is obvious. The peace of God is a result of adjustment to God's will and the experience of the fulness of the Spirit to perform that will. Such an experience, or even an attempt to enjoy such an experience, is a danger signal to Satan and immediately arouses his fierce attacks and subtle temptations. It is therefore quite apparent that the Christian who is afraid to face war against the devil will never know much of God's peace.

This does not mean, however, that all prayer is of the nature of a conflict, as in Ephesians 6:10-20. Philippians 4:6, 7 is clearly not of this character, and prayer is often an

34

exquisitely tranquil experience of converse with God, calm as a summer evening, quiet as an unruffled sea. But it does mean that it is impossible to be a Spirit-filled believer, and hence one who enjoys the peace of God, and not face the fury of the enemy. Believers who know little of the prayer conflict in Ephesians know little of "the peace of God" in Philippians.

The unsaved world, of course, knows nothing of peace with God or the peace of God. "The wicked are like the troubled sea, when it cannot rest, whose waters cast up mire and dirt. There is no peace, saith my God, to the wicked" (Isaiah 57:20, 21).

The anxiety that paralyzes the world need not affect the child of God, however. God desires to guard our hearts and minds against it. It is His gracious will that we walk undisturbed and undismayed through our earthly pilgrimage. However severe the storm *without* may be, the Christian must not allow it to get *within*. He must avail himself of the garrison God has set to guard his heart and mind against anxiety and fear. That garrison, which has never lost a battle nor suffered one fortress to be invaded or taken, is the peace of God. "And the peace of God, which passeth all understanding, shall guard your hearts and minds through Christ Jesus."

I. God's Peace Guards Against Care

There is no temptation that besets our hearts with more subtle danger than anxious care. It is a sin all the more inexcusable in a child of God because it is essentially the result of unbelief.

1. *The Curse of Care Is Terrific.* Nothing is so destructive of man's mental, physical and spiritual welfare as anxiety. Prolonged and excessive worry works havoc in men's minds, bodies and souls. Everywhere the shores of time are littered with its wreckage. The Lord Jesus repeatedly warned against its ravages, and used the birds of the heavens and the splendor

of flowered Palestinian hills in springtime to drive home the lesson to His hearers.

"Therefore, I say unto you, Take no thought for [don't be anxious about] your life, what ye shall eat, or what ye shall drink; nor yet for your body, what ye shall put on. Is not the life more than meat, and the body than raiment? Behold the fowls of the air: for they sow not, neither do they reap, nor gather into barns; yet your heavenly Father feedeth them. Are ye not much better than they? . . . And why take ye thought for [or, be anxious about] raiment? Consider the lilies of the field, how they grow; they toil not, neither do they spin: and yet I say unto you, That even Solomon in all his glory was not arrayed like one of these. Wherefore, if God so clothe the grass of the field, which to day is, and to morrow is cast into the oven, shall he not much more clothe you, O ye of little faith?" (Matthew 6:25-30).

2. *The Curse of Care Is Effective.* God's peace filling the soul is the only panacea for all the ills and perplexities that plague the human heart and mind. The apostle urges God's people to "be careful for nothing" (Philippians 4:6). In our common idiom he is saying, "Don't worry about anything!" But it is one thing to determine not to worry; it is quite another thing to be delivered from its scourge. It is, moreover, one thing not to worry about *some* things, quite another to worry about *nothing*. In any case the power of God in the human soul can accomplish the miracle.

God's peace is a *miracle*. It rises like a snow-capped peak above the valley of human reason and speculation. Its wonderful effectiveness will never be understood by the world. To the unspiritual mind it remains an unknown factor. God's Word specifically characterizes it as peace "which passeth all understanding" (Philippians 4:7). It is the invincible garrison God throws around the human heart to keep it intact against all besiegers.

II. God's Peace Is Realized By Prayer

"Be careful for nothing; but in every thing by prayer" (Philippians 4:6). Worry about *nothing*, but pray about *everything!* What we don't pray about we shall soon find ourselves worrying about. God's peace is the result of God's presence and power in the human soul. God manifests Himself as the result of prayer.

1. *Prayer Is Asking.* "By prayer . . . let your requests be made known unto God" (Philippians 4:6). The very term "prayer" in the original means a strong desire directed toward God. Prayer can mean little and be practiced less unless we have a keen sense of need. God welcomes the expression of that need in prayer. He does not promise to remove all our problems and difficulties. But He does guarantee that His deep, settled peace shall possess our souls and guard our hearts and minds through Christ Jesus.

This is exactly what we need. The poet expresses the thought in his petition:

> Take from our hearts the strain and stress,
> And let our ordered lives confess
> The beauty of Thy peace.
> —*John G. Whittier*

The "strain and stress"—not the burdens and difficulties—do the damage.

2. *Prayer Is Supplicating.* Prayer is frequently something more than mere asking. It is often prompted by a greater degree of urgency. Now and then we find ourselves facing some sudden emergency, like the man who came to his friend at midnight requesting loaves (Luke 11:5-10). But God is always equal to the emergency, and we are heard, if for no other reason, than because of our importunity.

3. *Prayer Is Thanksgiving.* "In every thing by prayer and supplication with thanksgiving let your requests be made known unto God" (Philippians 4:6). Prayer should *always* be largely thanksgiving because God gives so lavishly and His

grace is so indescribably bounteous. Yet how common is the sin of ingratitude! Too often we take the blessing for granted and forget to thank the Blesser. The disappointed words of our Saviour after He cleansed the ten lepers are still to be heard today: "Were there not ten cleansed? but where are the nine?" (Luke 17:17). Often the Heavenly Father's heart is pained by the unthankfulness of His children.

4. *Prayer Is Rewarding.* "Let your requests be made known . . ." (Philippians 4:6). As a mother loves to have her sobbing child tell her every trouble, and the difficulty is soothed away in mother's arms, so God delights to have us come to Him with the little perplexities of our daily lives as well as the big problems. Most of us have no hesitation about the big things. It is the little, seemingly insignificant matters we hesitate to bring to God, supposing He is not concerned about them.

All the while, however, we not only bear the burden of the little loads that amount in the end to a great weight of care, but we miss the exquisite intimacy with the Heavenly Father that the Christian enjoys who takes *everything* to God in prayer. Besides, he who takes all to God in holy interview finds that the divine presence throws such a defense around the citadel of His soul that He is kept by the power of God from all anxiety and care.

When we learn to cast ourselves more completely upon God's wonderful grace and accustom ourselves to cultivate the holy art of bringing every detail of our lives to Him in holy petition and praise, we shall more and more discover the deep tranquillity of the divine presence.

Are you perplexed, troubled, worried? Let God's peace guard *your* heart!

CHAPTER TWO

THE PATHWAY OF KNOWLEDGE

Meditating Upon God's Word

But his delight is in the law of the Lord; and in his law doth he meditate day and night (Psalm 1:2). *I have more understanding than all my teachers; for thy testimonies are my meditation* (Psalm 119:99).

MEDITATION upon God's Word is fast becoming a lost art among many Christian people. This holy exercise of pondering over the Word, chewing it as an animal chews its cud to get its sweetness and nutritive virtue into the heart and life, takes time, which ill fits into the speed of our modern age. Today most Christians' devotions are too hurried, their lives too rushed. But holiness and hurry never did suit well together. Prayer and preoccupation have always been strange bed-fellows. A head knowledge of the Word may perhaps be consonant with the scurry of the age, but not a deep heart experience of its preciousness. A deep knowledge of spiritual things can only come by the way of unhurried reflection upon God's truth and by prayer.

Once again we need to give earnest heed to the old hymn:

> Take time to be holy
> Speak oft with thy Lord,
> Spend much time in secret
> With Jesus your Lord.

The fervor of the ancient psalmist for the Word of God needs to grip our hearts today. "O how I love thy law, it is my meditation all the day" (Psalm 119:97). "How sweet are thy words unto my taste! yea, sweeter than honey to my

41

mouth!" (Psalm 119:103). "The judgments of the Lord are true and righteous altogether. More to be desired are they than gold, yea, than much fine gold: sweeter also than honey and the honeycomb" (Psalm 19:9, 10).

We need to heed the Lord's injunction to Joshua, "This book of the law shall not depart out of thy mouth; but thou shalt meditate therein day and night, that thou mayest observe to do according to all that is written therein: for then thou shalt make thy way prosperous, and then thou shalt have good success" (Joshua 1:8). Like Isaac who "went out to meditate in the field at the eventide" (Genesis 24:63), we need to cultivate the practice of holy reflection.

I. MEDITATING UPON GOD'S WORD INSURES SPIRITUAL PROSPERITY

The blessed man of Psalm 1 has "his delight in the law of the Lord; and in his law doth he meditate day and night." And he is said to be "like a tree planted by the rivers of water, that bringeth forth his fruit in his season; his leaf also shall not wither; and whatsoever he doeth shall prosper" (Psalm 1:2, 3).

1. *Meditation Upon God's Word Keeps Us From a Sinful and Harmful Life.* "Blessed is the man that walketh not in the counsel of the ungodly, nor standeth in the way of sinners, nor sitteth in the seat of the scornful" (Psalm 1:1). The happy man's blessedness is the result of his godliness. His godliness, which keeps him out of sin and the company of sinners and scoffers, is in turn the product of his constant meditation and delight in the Word of God. As the psalmist says, "Through thy precepts I get understanding: therefore I hate every false way" (Psalm 119:104).

Our Lord's statement to the disciples, "now ye are clean through the word which I have spoken unto you" (John 15:3) emphasizes the purifying power of the Word of God and the cleansing stream released in the human soul as a

result of meditation upon it. The Apostle Paul's reference likewise brings into focus the matchless purifying energy of the
Word. "Christ also loved the church, and gave himself for it;
that he might sanctify and cleanse it with the washing of
the water by the word" (Ephesians 5:25, 26).

2. *Meditation Upon God's Word Preserves Us For a
Righteous Useful Life.* The godly, happy man is bound to be
useful, if only to scatter sunshine. Holy, happy people exude
a glow and a warmth about them which have the same result
in the social realm as the warm spring sunshine has in the
realm of nature. The effect upon those who associate with
them is like the passing of winter's cold: "For lo the winter is
past; the rain is over and gone. The flowers appear on the
earth; the time of the singing of birds is come and the voice
of the turtle is heard in our land. The fig tree putteth forth
her green figs, and the vines with the tender grape give a
good smell" (Song of Solomon 2:11-13). Happy people in
this way are eminently useful in helping to thaw out unhappy
people. They act as a tonic and give a lift to their fellowman.

The godly happy man, who meditates in the Word of
God, is useful in other ways, too. "And he shall be *like a
tree.*" Few things in nature are lovelier and more useful than
a tree. Even when naked and leafless in the wintry sunshine,
it is a thing of charm. But when daintily bedecked with frost,
or robed in a mantle of snow, or garbed in spring's first faint
haze of green, or attired in summer's leafy loveliness or painted
with autumn's crimson and gold, a tree is a thing of superlative beauty. So is the child of God, who, meditating in the
Word of God, allows it to cleanse the depths of his soul and
produce in him the "beauty of holiness" (Psalm 110:3).

A part of the beauty of a tree and inseparable from it is
its utility. Whether giving protection from the pitiless summer
sun, or furnishing a choir loft and a home for the first spring
songsters, or wood to build man's abode, or food for man and
beast, the beauty of a tree is its utility. This, too, is the real

beauty of a Christian. A child of God is fairest when most useful, and is like his Master, who "went about doing good and healing all that were oppressed of the devil" (Acts 10:38).

The godly happy man, who meditates in the Word is useful, moreover, because he possesses a freshness and vitality that are a continual spring of inspiration to those who come in contact with him. "And he shall be like a tree *planted by the rivers of water,* whose leaf also shall *not wither.*" Rooted deep in God's truth, the Holy Spirit is to him a "well of water springing up into everlasting life" (John 4:14). Knowing the Scriptures and meditating on them, out of his innermost being "flow rivers of living water" (John 7:38).

The world to the Christian is a desert. His pilgrimage song is:

> I'm but a stranger here
> Heaven is my home.
> Earth is a desert drear,
> Heaven is my home.

While often colorful and fascinating like the world, the desert is a dangerous place — waterless, treeless, cheerless, characterized by weariness and barrenness, monotony and sameness, where death lurks at every turn in the scorching, shifting sands. Unsaved and ungodly people spiritually are like men lost in the desert, exhausted and tortured with thirst, having no knowledge of the water of life or of the rest and satisfaction afforded by the gospel of Christ.

Worldlings are frequently oppressed by the dullness and *ennui* of an empty round of activity for self and pleasure. Millions, who live only for the things of time and sense, can testify to the truth of the words of the ancient sage: "Vanity of vanities, saith the Preacher, vanity of vanities all is vanity" (Ecclesiastes 1:2). The "pleasures of sin" are only "for a season" (Hebrews 11:25). They soon lose their power to titillate and their ability to thrill. That which seemed at first sweet becomes bitter as wormwood. That which bid fair to be fresh and stimulating soon becomes stale and enervating.

The happy godly man meditating in the Word of God, by contrast, is ever delighted by the joy and the challenge of a full life of service for God's glory and man's blessing. Like a tree planted by the streams of water, his roots strike deep in the springs of God's power and grace. He finds true pleasures in glorifying God and serving his fellow man, which do not fade away or leave a bad taste in the mouth, but ever increase in delight and in supplying true satisfaction. His glad testimony is, "In thy presence is fulness of joy, at thy right hand there are pleasures forevermore" (Psalm 16:11).

Instead of becoming a victim of boredom like the ungodly man, as a life of easy self indulgence produces its inevitable harvest of staleness and disillusionment, the godly man is not only refreshed himself, but like a tree whose roots find the perennial stream of water, is able to refresh others. How many of God's children, growing in grace and in knowledge of the Lord Jesus through prayer and meditation in the Word of God, are like a tree "whose leaf also shall not wither." Under their spreading branches they supply shade in the desert where the children of men may find rest and refreshment from the burning heat.

The godly man also reaps another benefit from his meditation in the Word of God. "He bringeth forth his fruit in his season." He is not only like a beautiful and useful shade tree. He is like a fruit tree as well. Here again he is in striking contrast to the ungodly man, who yields neither fruit nor shade. In no phase of his life does the believer who meditates upon the Word bring more glory to God than in the matter of fruit-bearing. As Jesus said to His disciples, "Herein is my Father glorified, that ye bear much fruit; so shall ye be my disciples" (John 15:8).

The psalmist in concluding his graphic description of the godly man mentions one other happy result of his continual meditation in God's Word. "And whatsoever he doeth shall prosper." Often so much of the believer's activity is misdirected in effort and barren in result because it does not issue from holy worship and vital fellowship with God in prayer. The right kind of "doing" must be preceded by the right kind of "praying."

Too frequently prayer is a one-sided conversation with the suppliant doing all the talking. God is unconsciously excluded. Not until meditation upon the Word is made an intrinsic part of our devotions, in order that God may have opportunity to speak to us from His Word, will we be properly orientated in God's will and fully empowered by the Holy Spirit to perform it. And spiritual prosperity is nothing more than knowing God's will and completely discharging it by the power of the Holy Spirit. "Whatsoever" the godly man "doeth shall prosper" because by virtue of his meditation in God's Word he does only the will of God.

II. MEDITATING UPON GOD'S WORD SUPPLIES SPIRITUAL KNOWLEDGE

The psalmist's assertion that he had "more understanding" than all his teachers is not to be interpreted as a mere piece of youthful braggadocio, especially in the light of the reason he gives for his superior knowledge of spiritual things: "for thy testimonies *are my meditation*" (Psalm 119:99). The technical scholar, the purely intellectual expositor and the destructive higher critic, to whom prayerful meditation upon the Word of God in complete dependence upon the teaching and illumination of the Holy Spirit is foreign, are completely ignorant of simple spiritual truths and experiences that readily come to the child of God, who meditates in the Word under the tuition of God's Spirit.

1. *Meditating Upon God's Word Supplies Spiritual Knowledge of Man's Fall and Utter Depravity*. The evolutionary historian and the pseudo-scientific critic find the Biblical

revelation of the fall of man in Genesis 3 and Romans 1 a continual embarrassment to their theories of the development of culture and religious faith from lower to higher forms. For the same reason the self-righteous man finds the doctrine of man's total depravity and his utter dependence upon divine grace for salvation a stumbling block, and does not hesitate to reject it completely, as being thoroughly unpalatable. The godly man, who meditates in the Word and submits humbly to the Spirit's instruction, finds no barrier in these teachings to his salvation, but sees them verified in history and in his own human experience.

2. *Meditating Upon God's Word Supplies Spiritual Knowledge of Christ's Perfect Redemption.* Men are not ready to be saved until they see themselves lost. One of the very first lessons the Spirit teaches the honest heart, who meditates upon the Word, is the exceeding sinfulness of sin and the natural man's utterly lost estate (John 16: 8-10; Romans 7:13) apart from the saving work of Christ on the cross (II Corinthians 5:21). Convincing men of their lost condition the Spirit at the same time reveals to them the complete efficacy of the death of Christ and the perfect deliverance from the penalty and power of sin of those who trust in His redemptive work. Apart from the Spirit's operation men are not only blind to the reality of these truths, but blatantly deny them and hence cut themselves off from God's saving grace.

3. *Meditating Upon God's Word Supplies Spiritual Knowledge of the Divine Redemptive Program, Past, Present and Future.* The Apostle Paul had this benefit of meditation especially in mind when he wrote to young Timothy: "Study to shew thyself approved unto God, a workman that needeth not to be ashamed, rightly dividing the word of truth" (II Timothy 2:15). Only by diligent study coupled with prayerful dependence upon the Holy Spirit can God's dealings with humanity in the different ages be distinguished, and the great drama of redemption viewed in its beginning and ending with

the various intervening acts and scenes placed in their proper order. Only thus can our Lord Jesus Christ be seen as the great hero of the drama of the ages.

What is true with regard to comprehending God's plan and purpose for the ages is true also with regard to the believer's ascertaining the will of God for his own individual life. Waiting upon God in restful reflection upon the Word of God will disclose the mind of God. In the hour of quiet meditation the child of God will hear the voice of God saying, "This is the way, walk ye in it."

Vast and far-reaching are the benefits of meditating in the Word of God. The child of God who has learned to respond to God's Spirit calling him to his blessed duty will find himself saying concerning the Great Shepherd of the sheep: "He maketh me to lie down in green pastures: he leadeth me beside the still waters. He restoreth my soul: He leadeth me in the paths of righteousness for his name's sake" (Psalm 23:2, 3). May the Good Shepherd Himself cause us to take time, yea make time for the holy exercise of meditating in His Word.

Knowing God's Will

. . . Wherefore be ye not foolish, but understand what the *will of the Lord is* (Ephesians 5:17).

AN EXCEEDINGLY PRACTICAL PHASE of the believer's knowledge and that which has perhaps the closest bearing upon his power for effective Christian living concerns his understanding and doing the will of God. This subject also has a vital connection with meditating on the Word of God, which constitutes an important factor in ascertaining the will of God.

There is so much uncertainty, however, among God's people that the question, "Can I know I am in God's will?" may well be discussed. This is an exceedingly important matter to every believer, not only because real blessing to the Christian himself and to his fellow-man is involved in his adjustment to God's will, but God's glory in the life and testimony of the child of God is also vitally concerned. Outside the sphere of God's will the believer is seriously crippled and paralyzed insofar as his spiritual life and usefulness are concerned. The whole question takes on an added significance when the truth is realized that the will of God cannot be ascertained once and for all, but must be daily, even momentarily, sought.

The practical challenge, therefore, to the believer is: Am I in God's will now? Am I fully yielded to God? Have I made a full surrender? If so, am I now, today, living up to the terms of that surrender? Seeing then it is easy to miss God's will altogether, or having found it, lose it, it would be well first to ask ourselves the question

I. How Can We Know We Are Not In God's Will?

Several prominent symptoms point to the disease. We can easily diagnose our case.

1. *First There Is a Disposition to Folly.* We have a foolish desire to do things which are not according to God's Word, and hence, which are really to our hurt. The apostle closely connects this foolish course of action with ignorance concerning the will of God. "Wherefore, be *not foolish*, but understand what the will of the Lord is." How potent a preserver from folly a knowledge of the will of God is!

How easy for a Christian, falling out of step with God's marching orders, to marry an unbeliever, or leave the stern discipline of Christian education for easy money in the world. How readily we may fall in with the glitter and tinsel of worldly amusements and activities, and lose the fine touch of God upon the soul, become deaf to the heavenly vision and ignore the call to noble self-sacrificing service on the mission field or in the homeland. No one can so sadly play the role of a fool as that one who, blessed by the grace of God with salvation and the revelation of the divine will, loses the sense of God, and wanders in the quagmire of self-planning.

2. *There Is Inevitably a Condition of Leanness.* Having fully yielded to God and not daily living up to the contract, we may at any time lose the knowledge of God's will and a sense of God's presence, producing leanness of soul. By carelessness in our devotional life, by unconfessed sin, by worldliness, or more dangerously by deliberately lusting after our own will and pleasures until God gives us our desire, we may find ourselves seriously impoverished spiritually. This was the sin of the redeemed people of God in the Old Testament. "They lusted exceedingly in the wilderness, and tempted God in the desert. And he gave them their request, but *sent leanness into their soul*" (Psalm 106:14, 15).

Those who know the will of God and do it are never cursed with spiritual leanness. They flourish "like the palm tree." They grow "like a cedar in Lebanon." They are "planted in the house of the Lord" and "flourish in the courts of our God." "They shall still bring forth fruit in old age. They shall be fat and flourishing" (Psalm 92:12-14).

Spiritual leanness! How many and varied are the symptoms! Prayerlessness, neglect of the Bible, carnality, worldliness, selfishness, lack of interest in God's work and in witnessing. God permitted us to have something we yearned after, but which was not in His plan for us. The result? Spirtual leanness.

It is significant that the injunction to "be filled with the Spirit" (Ephesians 5:18) comes immediately after that concerning understanding the will of God. The two are inseparable. We can't know the fulness of the Spirit if we miss God's will.

3. *There Is Frequently an Experience of Darkness.* We experience prolonged turmoil, confusion and uncertainty. These elements may all be involved normally, preceding and during an important crisis of choice. But when we choose God's will decisively, clarity, peace and certainty soon come. Prolonged darkness and indecision are indicative that God's will has been missed or bypassed somewhere along the line.

II. How Can We Know We Are In God's Will?

Several prominent signs indicate spiritual health. We can easily check up on our vitality.

1. *There Will Be Conscious Contact with Christ.* Unmistakable evidences of full touch with the Son of God will appear. Tension and strain, which slay their tens of thousands, will vanish before the certainty that we are in conscious life-contact with the Holy Spirit. Instead of the darkness and gloom of self will come the radiant dawn and full daylight of His presence and manifest guidance. Instead of uncertainty and paralyzing indecision the glad shout will echo in our hearts, "I know Whom I have believed, and am persuaded that he is able to keep that which I have committed unto him

against that day" (II Timothy 1:12). Instead of our unrest, His peace. Instead of our flimsy happiness, His joy. Instead of a desert, a well-watered garden. Instead of nervous self-preoccupation, the fine poise of being occupied with Christ in the service of others.

God's will, so exquisitely real and wonderful, so easily missed, so easily lost, demands this daily moment-by-moment leading of Him whose will we seek. Lost contact with Him means the fading-out of the knowledge of His will. The contact *must* be preserved or the vision will fail. The plan will be by passed.

2. *There Will Be an Over plus of Grace.* In the will of God there will not only be grace to help us walk the strait and narrow way, but an amazing overflow of divine favor to tide us over difficulties and persecutions. Adjusted to the divine plan, the child of God discovers a fulness of divine favor at work. Whereas the ungodly and even carnal believers must have the glitter and tinsel of worldly pursuit and pleasure to bolster their living against boredom and ennui, the obedient child of God finds joy and deep satisfaction wholly without the artificial air of these worldly attractions and pastimes. Worldlings conclude erroneously that the Christian life is colorless, cramped and miserable. They are ignorant of God's superabounding grace which more than compensates for the loss of these apparently necessary elements of an enjoyable life.

3. *There Will Be Progressive Preparation and Usefulness.* In God's will the Spirit of God not only prepares us, but uses us for God's glory while we are being prepared. There is no chance occurrence in God's plan. Things fit. The pattern at the moment may seem mixed up like a jig-saw puzzle. But the pieces form a plan. Time and patience are necessary. The pattern will appear. The perfect picture will result. Meanwhile, as divine wisdom puts the pieces to-

gether, we must trust His infinite skill and grace to bring out the pattern. *He will!* He *never* fails.

It is comforting to know, also, that while He is preparing our lives, He is all the while graciously using us to bring blessing and the light of salvation to a suffering and distraught world that *needs Him!* We may not always be aware that He is using us, but He is! It is impossible to be in contact with the living Christ and not give out the blessing and inspiration of that contact. They took notice of the early Christians that "they had been with Jesus" (Acts 4:13).

Can I know I'm in God's will? Most assuredly I can. If I am not in His will, the symptoms are plain — a disposition to folly, a condition of leanness, and an experience of darkness. I can diagnose my trouble. If I am in His will, the signs of health are apparent — conscious contact with Christ, over-plus of grace, progressive preparation and continually increasing usefulness. May this glad fact that *I can know* inspire us not only *to know,* but also *to do* the will of God.

Forgetting Past Failures

. . . Forgetting those things which are behind (Philippians 3:13).

IF THE SPIRITUAL KNOWLEDGE the believer acquires in meditating upon God's Word and finding God's will is to be the medium of the greatest blessing and power, he must learn how to forget certain things as well as to remember others. Most of us readily realize the great value of remembering, but we frequently fail to see the benefits of forgetting. Yet to forget is at times quite as important as to remember.

However, it is not always easy to forget, that is, to forget what we ought to forget. Most of us are only too well aware of our weakness in forgetting what we ought to remember. But to forget what we ought to forget is an art. Like any other art, it must be learned and cultivated by diligent study and persistent practice.

Acquiring the art of forgetting is important in any realm of life, but particularly in the spiritual. Spiritual progress in a definite sense depends upon our being able to forget the past. Multitudes cannot go forward because they are continually held backward by the past. Many are slaves in a world where they might be free men because they are chained by the past. Millions daily suffer the torments of hell because they *cannot* forget the past, which rises up like a lurid spectre to haunt them with its bitter memories of sin. There are those who would give all they possess to have their previous record blotted out with its ugly stain of guilt and its dismal failure.

I. WE MUST FORGET THE PAST

Deliverance from the past, however, can only come through Christ. He alone is the answer to the past as well as the present and the future. He only can forgive our sins, blot out the past, overrule our failure, and give us a challenging present and a glorious future. He alone can enable us to forget the past because He deals with the sin and failure that make the past so intolerable.

It was because the apostle knew the saving power of Christ himself and proclaimed that power to others that he could not only offer himself as an example of one who had been delivered from the past, but point out the way of deliverance to his hearers. He himself knew the art of forgetting and was therefore able to teach it to others. The lesson is simple, but none the less indispensable, to the welfare of the people of God.

1. *We Must Forget Past Failures.* The apostle did not let the sins and blunders he committed before he met Christ on the Damascus road blunt the keen edge of his zeal for the Saviour. The sad spectacle of his breathing out threatenings and slaughter against the disciples of the Lord, the painful scene when he held the garments of those who stoned Stephen — all the old life of blindness and bigotry — was under the blood. God had graciously blotted it out, and the apostle determined not to call it back to hinder concentration of life and purpose upon Jesus Christ. "This *one* thing I do, forgetting those things which are behind, and reaching forth unto those things which are before, I press toward the mark for the prize of the high calling of God in Christ Jesus" (Philippians 3:13, 14).

There was an amazing concentration of spiritual energy in Paul's life. He jealously guarded it against distraction by preoccupation with past sin and failure. He had learned the immensely valuable secret, which so many of God's people need to learn, that occupation with Christ is the only way to be liberated from the tyranny of sin and its tantalizing power. He was able to do the "one thing" of glorifying God in the present because he had learned how to forget the many distractions of the past.

2. *We Must Forget Past Successes*. It is not sufficient to forget only past failures. If we learn the art of forgetting well, as Paul did, we shall perceive the wisdom of forgetting past successes as well. In order to keep pressing on toward the goal it is just as important to forget past successes as failures — not, of course, in the sense of being ungrateful for God's blessing enabling us to glorify Him, but in the sense of resting in past achievement.

Not Paul! He had seen the resurrected Christ on the Damascus road. But he was not resting in that glorious experience. He was caught up "even to the third heaven . . . into Paradise, and heard things which it is not lawful for a man to utter" (II Corinthians 12:2, 3). But he did not allow that experience, as wonderful as it was, to sidetrack him into thinking he had attained all there was to attain or to give up the race, and cease pressing on toward the goal. The apostle's words are solemn. "Brethren, I count not myself to have apprehended (laid hold)" (Philippians 3:13). He had climbed high, but as far as he was concerned, there were loftier crags ahead where he had not yet set foot. He had run fleetly, but there was the home stretch in the course he had not yet run. The highest prize for superlative performance was still ahead. The call was still, "Onward!"

He had carried the Gospel from one end of the Roman Empire to the other, founding churches and establishing Christianity in the heart of Greek and Roman paganism. But he did not lie back on his laurels. The magnificent passion surging through his soul impelled him ever forward with restless energy to preach the Gospel where Christ was not named (Romans 15:20). Neither failure nor success could deter the apostle from an unflagging love for Christ and an all-out devotion to his cause.

II. We Must Remember That Our Opportunity for Achievement Lies in the Present

Forgetting past failures and successes is not an end in itself. The art of forgetting is merely the means to an end. It prepares the way for that which is its purpose; namely, to enable us undisturbed and undistracted to press on in Christian achievement.

1. *We Must Remember to Press Forward.* This was the apostle's reason for forgetting the past. It must likewise be our motive. "Forgetting those things which are behind, and reaching forth to those things which are before, I *press toward* the mark . . ." (Philippians 3:13, 14).

This is the thing of superlative value that makes the Christian life grand beyond description and grander and more challenging as it progresses. "Reaching forth unto those things which are before." And everything worthwhile lies before — heaven, immortality, victory, glory and fadeless joy. Nothing but defeat and despair lie behind.

Little wonder the apostle sees the Christian life as a runner in a foot race with every nerve and muscle keyed to the highest pitch and all the fine energy of mind and body concentrated on reaching the goal. This is the concentration of spiritual energy that wins. There is no time for looking back. No time to be a quitter.

2. *We Must Remember to Keep Our Eye on the Goal Set Before Us.* The goal is the upward calling of all those vitally joined to the Son of God and who will share His glory throughout eternity. "I press toward the mark for the prize of the high calling of God in Christ Jesus" (Philippians 3:14).

Paul visualized the judgment seat of Christ when rewards would be dispensed to those who lived in this present world as believers whose "citizenship" was in heaven (Philippians 3:20), who walked worthily of the vocation wherewith they were called (Ephesians 4:1), who, as those joined to Christ in the heavenlies, set their affections on things above and not on things on the earth, realizing they died and their life "was hid with Christ in God," and that when Christ would appear, they would also be manifested with Him in glory (Colossians 3:1-4).

The apostle ever aimed to translate his glorious position in Christ into an ever joyous and victorious experience of Christ, and he permitted nothing to distract him from concentrating spiritual energy toward the accomplishment of this lofty goal. He learned how to forget the past — its successes as well as its failures. He learned how to remember that opportunity for holy achievement lay in the present. He disciplined himself to seize every opportunity for good and for God by continually pressing forward with eye fixed unswervingly on his high calling in union with Christ. May we follow his noble example.

Learning the art of forgetting will take care of the past as we yield ourselves to Christ. The present is as bright as the promises of God. The future lies like a golden continent of opportunity ahead unoccupied, untouched. It is our land of splendid opportunity and conquest through Christ. There remaineth yet "very much" of it "to be possessed" (Joshua 13:1). Let us go in and possess it!

> Lead on, O King Eternal,
>   We follow, not with fears,
> For gladness breaks like morning
>   Where'er Thy face appears;
> Thy cross is lifted o'er us;
>   We journey in its light:
> The crown awaits the conquest;
>   Lead on, O King of might.
>   —*Ernest W. Surtleff*

Understanding What the Christian Life Is

For to me to live is Christ . . . (Philippians 1:21). I have been crucified with Christ; and it is no longer I that live, but Christ liveth in me . . . (Galatians 2:20).

A MOST IMPORTANT PHASE of the believer's knowledge is contained in the question: What is the Christian life? To many this query might seem so simple and elementary as not to merit serious attention. Yet when one considers the misunderstanding which prevails even among otherwise well-instructed Christians when an answer to this question is asked, not to mention the hopelessly confused and fantastic notions which are current among professing Christians in general, the urgent necessity for a clear and precise Scriptural answer becomes apparent. The need is accentuated by the exceedingly practical nature of the consideration. Can we live the Christian life if we do not know exactly what the Christian life is? Indeed, what is perhaps more disconcerting, can we lay any assured claim to being a Christian at all, if we are hazy in our thinking as to what a Christian is?

Is it sufficient to lay claim to the Christian life (as multitudes do) on the basis of some external rite, church membership, or human morality, or is there something deeper and more fundamental to the experience? Is the common notion that the Christian life consists in following Christ's example valid? Is the Christian life essentially an imitation? Can human nature by its own strength imitate Christ? Are we by self-effort, by our own works and human strivings to overcome sin, and thereby live as Christ lived? Nay, these

59

widespread but faulty ideas of the Christian life we must reject as unscriptural.

When we go to the Scripture itself, we find that the Christian life from beginning to end is a divine miracle. It begins in the miracle of the new birth (John 3:3), is sustained by the miracle of the energizing Spirit (Galatians 5:16), and is lived by the miracle of the indwelling Christ (Galatians 2:20, Philippians 1:21). It will consummate in the miracle of glorification, when we see Christ, and are made like Him (I John 3:2). Hence the Christian life is something beyond our poor strivings and our paltry efforts. It is, as the apostle says, "not I, but Christ."

That this is the Christian life, and that nothing short of it will satisfy the definitions of God's Word appears from a threefold consideration. First, from a consideration of God's requirement; second from a realization of our failure; and third, from a comprehension of God's provision.

I. God's Requirement for the Christian Life Is Supernatural

1. *His Requirement Is Dictated By His Divine Standard.* Human goodness, fleshly works, natural morality, and man-made criteria will not stand here! It is God's realm. God's norm must be considered. God's standard must be met. He bids us soar, but no human wings can lift us. He bids us ascend the heights where the air is pure and bracing and the vision is lofty, but our own unaided strength is totally unequal to the climb. His criterion calls not for a superman, but rather a "God-indwelt, Spirit-energized man."

He says, "Love your enemies." But we have difficulty sometimes to love even our friends. He says, "Rejoice always." But many Christians find it possible to rejoice only upon occasion. He says, "Don't worry about anything." But we are prone to worry about everything. He says, "Walk as Jesus walked." But we find our wayward feet ceaselessly straying from the path of duty.

Why, then, does the Lord, so tender, so wise, so sympathetically understanding, not make the requirement more in keeping with human nature? Why does He seem to be so unreasonable?

2. *His Requirement Is Designed to Produce a Human Dilemma.* God's purpose is not to be arbitrary or unreasonable. He would convince us of our sinfulness that we might accept His forgiveness. He would persuade us of our inability that we might avail ourselves of His ability. He would cleanse and empower us to meet His standard, rather than lower His standard to our defilement and weakness. He would prove to us the utter worthlessness of the flesh, that we might walk by the Spirit. He would demonstrate to us the exceeding sinfulness of sin, that we might trust ever and only in the finished work of Christ.

Moreover, is there any point in avoiding the dilemma, which God has purposely created? Is anything to be gained by subterfuge, pretending that the gulf between the humanly possible and what God requires is, after all, not so great? Of course not! What greater boon could possibly come to us than that we should see ourselves utterly lost and undone apart from Christ so that we might flee to His redemptive work as our only plea? And having fled to the ark of safety, what more liberating and rest-giving truth could set our spirits free than that we should see the utter futility of our own poor strivings and contaminated works to please Him Who has saved us by His grace, and that, in consequence, we should cast ourselves wholly upon the power and the resources of God to enable us to live the Christian life?

II. OUR FAILURE IN THE CHRISTIAN LIFE IS COMPLETE

1. *Failure on the Part of the Unregenerate to Live the Christian Life Is Due to the Effects of the Fall.* No deception

is quite so pathetic as that which allows a man to be religious but unsaved, and to have a form of godliness but to deny the power. No epitaph could be more heart-rending than, "Religious, but lost!" Yet the appalling tragedy of our day, as we advance more and more into the period of the Laodicean Church of the last days (Revelation 3:17, 18), is that the exceeding sinfulness of sin is denied, the lost condition of the human race in Adam is laughed at, and the supreme necessity of the finished work of Christ is disbelieved. Men are assured that human morality is sufficient, and that there is no need for a divine Saviour crucified for the sins of a fallen race. Forms, ceremonies and mere human accomplishments are substituted for repentance, faith and regeneration. We are living in a day when the term Christian is getting more and more to mean less and less. God's Word, however, stands like a bulwark, assuring us that all Adam's sons are "under sin" (Romans 3:9) and need a divine crucified and risen Saviour from sin (Romans 3:26).

2. *Failure on the Part of the Regenerate to Live the Christian Life as It Should Be Lived Is Due to the Defilement of the Old Nature.* In the light of God's supernatural standard our failure as Christians is all too familiar to us. Too often we live in the defeat and despair of the seventh chapter of Romans rather than in the calm assured victory of the eighth. Why? We fail to see the complete worthlessness of self, and the thoroughgoing defilement of the old nature. We feel, somehow, we can live the Christian life ourselves.

Too often we fail to get to the place of self-confessed defeat, where we cry out, "I can't!" and own, "O wretched man that I am! Who shall deliver me?" (Romans 7:24). But there is scant hope of believing "He does" till we cry out the double confession: "I can't, but He can!" Not until we see that we live the Christian life in exactly the same way we began the Christian life; namely, *by looking away completely from our ownselves, and fastening our faith solely upon the resources and the power of God.* Not till we do this will the victory be ours!

III. GOD'S PROVISION FOR THE CHRISTIAN LIFE IS PERFECT

1. *His Provision Procures Freedom from the Penalty and the Power of Sin.* The penalty, which entails wrath and eternal hell, is remitted once-for-all and forever the moment faith is reposed in the finished work of Christ. We are "justified freely by His grace through the redemption that is in Christ Jesus" (Romans 3:24). This glorious transformation takes place in our hearts the moment we believe the good news, which says, "Christ died *for me!*" But there is another aspect of the Gospel, as potent in delivering the child of God from the *power* of sin as the message, "Christ died for me!" is instrumental in rescuing the sinner from the penalty of sin. It is the glorious, but oft-neglected truth, "I died *in Christ!*" In the mind and reckoning of God, I died to the old life of sin and shame in Adam, because when I believed on Christ, the last Adam, I was baptized into vital union with Him by the Holy Spirit (Romans 6:3, 4), so that I am now set free from the bondage of sin.

2. *His Provision Implies Identification in His Death.* "For by one Spirit we were all baptized into one body . . ." (I Corinthians 12:13). The moment I believe on Him as my Saviour from the penalty of sin, I am made one with Him, and one with all other believers in Him. The body of Christ is one! Many members, but only one body! And the body, with its many members, is vitally and eternally joined to the living, directing Head—Christ! The members of the body, joined by the Holy Spirit to the Head, share the death of the Head (Romans 6:3, 4). "Ye died . . ." (Colossians 3:3). "One died for all, therefore all died" (II Corinthians 5:14).

Nothing separates quite so effectually as death. Death severs a person completely from this earthly life and all its

connections. Death frees a woman from the law of her hus-
band (Romans 7:3). Likewise identification with Christ in
His death separates us from sin, self and the old creation in
Adam, and places us in the new creation in Christ. This is
our position in the mind and reckoning of God. It becomes
our real and vital experience as we reckon it so. It is by faith
we reckon it so, and it is thus by faith that we gain victory
over the power of sin, as it is by faith we were delivered from
the penalty of sin. The Christian life is accordingly to be
lived by faith, as it was begun in faith. It is "from faith"
(beginning in faith) "unto faith" (ending in faith) (Romans
1:17) with every step between by faith.

3. *His Provision Provides Participation in the Power of
His Resurrection.* Not only did we die in Christ — in Him
we arose! The same power that raised Jesus from the dead
is at our disposal to give us victory over the power of sin.
Our "death position" makes possible our "resurrection position." Moreover, our "death-resurrection position" is true
whether we reckon it to be true or not. The difference is
when we reckon it true it becomes experimentally real. The
reckoning is simply believing to be true what the Word of
God says about our *position in Christ* and acting upon that
position (Romans 6:11).

Thus the Christian life is Christ. He is not only the
center and source of our life. He *is* our life (Colossians
3:4). As we *believe* He is what He is to us, and we are
what we are in Him, His own radiant, joyous, triumphant,
resurrection life is manifested in our experience. This is
normal Christianity. This, and nothing less than this, is the
Christian life, nurtured, sustained and manifested by faith in
the Son of God.

This glowing truth shines out in full radiance, like a
rich many-faceted jewel, in the words of the apostle: "I have
been crucified with Christ (our death position); and it is no
longer I that live (our death position), but Christ liveth in me

(our resurrection position): and that life which I now live in the flesh (the *normal* Christian life) I live in faith, the faith which is in the Son of God (the key to *experiential* realization), who loved me, and gave himself up for me" (the basis of our position and our experience) (Galatians 2:20).

Is this life, ours by right of our position in union with our blessed Lord, also ours in thrilling experience? Are we possessing our possessions in Christ? Or do we go on as paupers when we are made princes, possessing the wealth of heaven? Are we in the place of slaves, when it is ours to enjoy the freedom and privileges of sons? May God grant us wisdom not only to understand what the Christian life is, but also faith to appropriate its full power and blessing!

> This is my wonderful story,
>   Christ to my heart has come;
> Jesus, the King of Glory,
>   Finds in my heart a home.
>
> Christ in me, Christ in me,
>   Christ in me, wonderful story,
> Christ in me, Christ in me,
>   Christ in me, hope of glory.
>
> Now in His bosom confiding,
>   This my glad song shall be;
> I am in Jesus abiding,
>   Jesus abides in me.
>   —*A. B. Simpson*

Learning Christ

"But ye have not so learned Christ . . ." (Ephesians 4:20).

In the letter to the Ephesians the Apostle Paul by the Spirit employs an expression unique in all literature, and one which presents a phase of knowledge vital to the power and progress of the believer: "But ye have not so *learned Christ*" (Ephesians 4:20). "*Learning Christ!*" What does the apostle mean? We are accustomed to the expression "learning *about* people." But the phrase "to learn a person" is altogether unusual. Indeed, the usage is only possible at all because the person to be learned is altogether unusual. The Lord Jesus is the Unique One *par excellence*. Never has there been one like Him. Never shall there be one like Him. His soul shall ever be "a star that dwells apart."

Our blessed Lord is not only the school in which the Christian is instructed, He is the lesson the Christian is taught. He is the message the Christian receives. Being a Christian is not learning *about* Christ. We may know all about the life of Christ and yet not be a Christian. Being a Christian is not learning *about* the Bible. We may know the Bible by heart and still be unsaved. Being a Christian, however, is *learning Christ,* becoming vitally acquainted with His glorious Person.

Christ is not merely the founder of our religion. He *is* our religion. Christianity *is* Christ. Professing Christians who do not learn Christ, no matter how much they may learn *about* Him, are not Christians at all. To be regenerated is to learn Christ in His saving, cleansing power. To be conformed

66

to His image is to learn Christ as our Lord and Master, our All in All, the One Altogether Lovely, the Fairest of Ten Thousand to the soul. To be Spirit-filled and victorious in our Christian experience is to learn Christ as our Deliverer, our Victor, the Captain of our salvation.

Christ is purity, the exact opposite of the corruption of the world. When we learn Him, He saves us unto all that He is and from all that He is not. It is impossible to learn Him and walk and live as formerly we did. A Christian is entirely "a new creation." "Old things have passed away: behold, *all things* are become new" (II Corinthians 5:17).

So important is the matter of "learning Christ" we may well ask ourselves precisely what it means.

I. LEARNING CHRIST MEANS WE HAVE PUT OFF THE OLD LIFE OF SIN

Since "learning Christ" denotes a genuine experience of Christ's salvation, it also means that the believer has been baptized by the Holy Spirit into vital union with Christ—into His death and resurrection (Romans 6:3, 4). Consequently, he is "in Christ" and in the mind and reckoning of God has put off the "old man" and put on the new. This is the believer's unchanging position. His enjoyment of this glorious position in actual experience depends upon his faith to reckon himself "dead indeed unto sin" (i.e. to have "put off the old man") and "alive unto God" (i.e. to have "put on the new man") (Romans 6:11, Ephesians 4:22, 24). In proportion as he reckons upon the fact that he has put off the old and put on the new will he enjoy the *experiential reality* of deliverance from the old life.

1. *The Old Life We Have Put Off Is a Life of Vanity.* Nothing more broadly characterizes the unconverted world than the term "vanity." Solomon, draining the world's alluring cup of pleasure and self-indulgence and finding the dregs bitter could only exclaim, "Vanity of vanities . . . all is vanity"

(Ecclesiastes 1:2). The apostle warns against the same empty purposelessness that is descriptive of all activity and endeavor that leave God out of consideration. "This I say, therefore, and testify in the Lord, that ye henceforth walk not as other Gentiles walk, in the *vanity* of their mind" (Ephesians 4:17).

Notice, nothing is said in this connection about gross wickedness or immorality — simply about an empty or purposeless attitude of mind. Man's mind is a marvelous endowment of the Creator. With it he thinks and knows. Yet how many waste their God-given intellectual faculties in useless and often harmful pleasures or prostitute their talents on worldly pursuits and selfish interests. How many worldly people, even believers, are without purpose or worthwhile aim in life, victims of purposeless vain living, like a ship adrift upon the sea of time without rudder or pilot. Learning Christ, who is both rudder and pilot, alone can truly orientate the soul and give worthwhile purpose to life.

2. *The Old Life We Have Put Off Is a Life of Darkness.* The apostle describes the experience of unconverted people not only as walking "in the vanity of their mind" but also as "having the understanding darkened." He does not for a moment mean to imply that the unsaved may not be brilliant intellectually and highly educated. But he does mean that being afflicted with moral and spiritual darkness, a sin for which salvation has been provided, they cannot know God or understand "the truth" as it is "in Jesus" (Ephesians 4:21). Learning Him Who is "the Way, the Truth, and the Life" (John 14:6) is the only escape from "the god of this world" who "hath blinded the minds of them which believe not, lest the light of the glorious, gospel of Christ, Who is the image of God, should shine unto them" (II Corinthians 4:4).

3. *The Old Life We Have Put Off Is a Life of Alienation.* "Being alienated from the life of God" (Ephesians 4:18)

is the apostle's terse description. The "life of God" in the soul produces moral and spiritual health. Separation from that life constitutes intellectual and moral corruption. Learning Christ as the Life-Giver alone can quicken us "who were dead in trespasses and sins" (Ephesians 2:1).

Two reasons are named by the apostle for this estrangement from the life of God—ignorance and blindness (hardening) of heart. His words are incisive—"being alienated from the life of God through the ignorance that is in them because of the blindness of their heart" (Ephesians 4:18). Ignorance takes its appalling toll in every realm, especially in the spiritual, where in a day of boasted enlightenment it has reached colossal proportions. Multitudes are better posted on the latest developments in baseball than on the plain facts of the Bible. The average person today knows more about the latest movie stars than about Moses.

Yet ignorance is almost always inexcusable, particularly, as in our day, when there is ample opportunity for enlightenment. Nor does it exempt its multitudinous victims from penalty. Just as the person who is ignorant of common health laws, and who carelessly or deliberately exposes himself to infection, contracts the disease notwithstanding, so the person who carelessly or wilfully remains ignorant of God's salvation in Christ, suffers the consequences of sin here and now and the torments of hell hereafter.

The second cause of estrangement from the life of God mentioned by the apostle is everywhere observable. Hardening of the heart is the natural result of excluding God from the life. Man's high prerogative of being able to say *yes* or *no* to God, like every other exalted privilege, is fraught with the gravest responsibility. He may say *no*, it is true, but each time he does so, it becomes more difficult to say *yes*, until finally his heart becomes so calloused he reaches that deplorable state ominously described as "being past feeling" (Ephesians 4:19) when all the overtures of God's grace fall upon deaf ears and strike not a single responsive chord — when all feeling of sorrow or remorse, of right or wrong, of morality or immorality vanishes, and when even conscience itself becomes silenced, "seared as with a hot iron."

4. *The Old Life We Have Put Off Is a Life of Shame.* This is the final downward step in man's apostasy — from vanity of mind, moral and spiritual darkness, and alienation from the life of God to profligacy and shamelessness of conduct. Hardness and indifference of heart are bound to lead to hardness and indifference in morals. "Who being past feeling have given themselves over unto lasciviousness, to work all uncleanness with greediness" (Ephesians 4:19).

It is a dismal picture of man's degeneracy. Enchained by unbridled lust, rebelling against all restraint, man not only abandons himself to depravity to satisfy his own passions, but makes a business or trade of vice to enrich himself at the expense of others' weakness. And the sin which he follows "with greediness" torments him. While it draws him on with ever-increasing desire, it never satisfies him. At the same time it lures him on to the precipice of destruction.

Such is God's picture of the pagan unconverted world, whether veneered with the culture and refinement of civilization, as here in America, or stripped of these outward embellishments and appearing in all its stark and hideous crudity among bushmen or aborigines of the jungle. It begins with a vain mind and descends to the lowest and grossest sins.

In striking contrast to the old life of sin, God's Word presents a picture of the new life of righteousness in Christ.

II. LEARNING CHRIST MEANS WE HAVE PUT ON THE NEW LIFE OF RIGHTEOUSNESS

When we took Christ as our Saviour, we put off the old life of sin as a filthy garment and put on the new life of righteousness as a spotless robe of white. And let us never forget if we are truly "in Christ" *God sees us only in the spotless robe of white.* The foul garments of the old life of sin have been forever removed from His eyes by our acceptance of the finished work of Christ.

Our enjoyment of walking in the unspotted garments down here in a world of sin, however, depends upon our reckoning ourselves to be so clothed. But our failure thus to reckon, does not render us any the less so clothed as far as God is concerned. It *does hinder us from enjoying the experimental reality of it.*

1. *The New Life We Have Put On Is a Life of Spiritual Renewal.* "That ye put off . . . the old man . . . and that ye put on the new man" (verses 22, 24) and *"be renewed in the spirit of your mind"* (verse 23). Instead of the vanity of mind in which the unconverted walk the Christian has his mind so animated by the Spirit of God that he is continually set aglow with new and vigorous life — giving power and purpose to all his thoughts and occupations. What a contrast to the old life! In the life of sin there is no renewal or rejuvenation, but only deterioration and corruption. The difference is in "learning Christ." "But ye have not so learned Christ if so be ye have heard him, and have been taught by him, as the truth is in Jesus" (verses 21, 22).

2. *The New Life We Have Put On Is a Life of Righteousness.* "And that ye put on the new man, which after God is created in righteousness" (verses 24). The "new man" is the regenerate personality which has become partaker of the divine nature. The "new man" is righteous because he is not the old man renovated or made over, but an entirely new work of God, "created in righteousness."

3. *The New Life We Have Put On Is a Life of True Holiness.* The "new man" is not only created after God "in righteousness" but also in "true holiness" (verse 24). There is a false and a true holiness. The one is a legalistic asceticism, the result of mere human effort. The other is a spontaneous

manifestation of the life of God in the human soul, the result of the Holy Spirit's presence.

In the regenerate life in which the old life is reckoned as put off, the new life is manifested in the fulness and power of the Holy Spirit. The negative gives way to the positive. Puny human effort is superseded by divine power. Instead of coldness, radiance. Instead of repulsion, attraction. Instead of defeat, victory. Instead of ashes, beauty. Instead of self, Christ.

This is "learning Christ" — whom to know as Saviour is life, whom to know as Lord is fulness of life, whom to know in ever-increasing intimacy and love is the gateway to fulness of power and blessing.

> I know not why God's wondrous grace
>   To me He hath made known,
> Nor why unworthy — Christ in love
>   Redeemed me for His own.
>
> But "I know whom I have believed,
>   And am persuaded that He is able
> To keep that which I've committed
>   Unto Him against that day."
>
> —*El Nathan*

CHAPTER THREE

THE PATHWAY OF FAITH

Meeting Trials and Testings

And it came to pass after these things, that God did test Abraham (Genesis 22:1, Hebrew). *By faith Abraham, when he was tested, offered up Isaac* (Hebrews 11:17, Greek).

"God did *test* Abraham." That is an amazing statement, full of comfort and encouragement for you and me. If God tested the great representative believer, may I not expect Him to test me? If he who was called "the Friend of God" (James 2:23) and "the father of all them that believe" (Romans 4:11), was severely tried, should I be surprised as a believer if trials and tribulations come to me? Certainly not. I must not only expect them to come, but meet them with faith and fortitude when they do come. The Apostle James goes a step farther and urges us to receive them with joy. "My brethren, count it all joy when ye fall into divers temptations; knowing this, that the trying of your faith worketh patience" (James 1:2, 3).

The life of Abraham and the experience of every true believer are similar to pursuing a course of study in school or college. There are lessons to be learned, discipline to be cultivated, and periodic tests and examinations to be passed. No one is exempt who enrolls in the school. As there are tests and examinations in school life, so there are tests and examinations in the Christian life. Abraham's spiritual experience consists of a series of such tests in which his faith was tried. This last test, when he was called upon to offer up Isaac, his "only son Isaac," was the greatest, and may fittingly be considered his *final* examination.

For this hardest test of all however, God had graciously prepared his ancient servant, as he tenderly prepares us. He gives the easier tests first, and like a skillful teacher, accommodates the examination to the maturity and advancement of the student. Faith in God is the indispensable prerequisite for passing the tests. God operates on the principle of faith. Without faith it is impossible to deal with Him or to please Him (Hebrews 11:6). We shall fail miserably in the Christian life if we do not believe God. We must constantly remember that the Christian life is a life of faith, that the life of faith is tested, that obedience is the test of faith, and that God *always* rewards obedience.

I. THE CHRISTIAN LIFE IS A LIFE OF FAITH

1. *The Christian Life Is Begun in Faith*. It is appalling to see how this most vitally important issue involving eternal destiny is confused and beclouded in the thinking and experience of many professing believers. Satan does his best to divert the soul from resting its case *solely* in the merits and the finished work of a crucified and risen Redeemer. He suggests that simple faith in Christ is not sufficient, or even necessary at all. If he cannot turn the soul completely away from Christ, he will resort to the next best makeshift and cause us to imagine we must add something to the finished redemption on the Cross.

How often works, morality, baptism, church membership or some other issue, good and right in its proper place, is introduced to confuse the way of salvation and made to serve in whole or in part as a substitute for simple faith in the full sufficiency of Christ's atoning work. Accordingly, the glorious truth that the Christian life is *begun in faith* in the Son of God (Ephesians 2:8, 9) is obscured.

2. *The Christian Life Is Lived By Faith*. It is just as impossible to live the Christian life as it is to begin the Christian life on any other basis than faith. "The gospel of Christ"

is the "power of God unto salvation to everyone that *believeth* . . . for therein is the righteousness of God revealed *from faith* (beginning in faith) *to faith* (ending in faith) (Romans 1:16, 17). Normal Christian living, which is victorious Christian living, is "Christ living in us." Such a life is lived "in faith, the faith which is in the Son of God," who loved us and gave Himself for us (Galatians 2:20 R.V.).

Abraham began his spiritual life by faith. "He believed in the Lord: and he counted it to him for righteousness" (Genesis 15:6). Moreover, Abraham lived a life well-pleasing to God, *by faith,* as we must do. His life, like that of all believers, consisted of a series of well-defined crises or turning points, in which he had to make a decisive choice by faith.

Four of these crises stand out like mountain peaks in his spiritual growth. First, "the God of glory" appeared unto him "when he was in Mesopotamia" (Acts 7:2). It was not easy to leave the great metropolis and commercial center of Ur for a strange and unknown land. But by faith God's ancient servant went forth "knowing not whither he went." The same call often comes to believers today to leave home, loved ones and country for some foreign field of service.

Secondly, God called His servant to separate from his ambitious and carnal nephew Lot, and to make the unselfish choice of faith (Genesis 13:5-18), as God calls us to separate from sinners and frequently from compromising believers. Later God called him to give up his own cherished plan concerning Ishmael, as God speaks to us to surrender cherished ambitions and desires in life contrary to His will. Finally, God called His renowned servant to make the supreme sacrifice of his life. "Take now thy son, thine only son Isaac, whom thou lovest . . . and offer him . . . for a burnt-offering" (Genesis 22:2). All of these momentous choices, especially the last, required faith in God and God's Word.

II. THE LIFE OF FAITH IS TESTED

1. *The Life of Faith Is of Such a Nature That It Must Be Tested.* Only by examination can the reality of faith be determined. "Faith without works is dead" (James 2:26), that is, is non-existent. Obedience, producing works, proves our faith. Like Abraham, every believer's life is a "school of faith," in which the Teacher, the Holy Spirit, teaches us lessons of faith. Every now and then God gives His pupils a test, a "term exam" or perhaps a "final examination" to see how well they are progressing in learning the lessons of faith.

2. *God Suits the Test to the Student's Advancement.* The simpler quizzes had been given and passed. Now God's tried and tested servant is ready for the "final examination." It is a difficult trial, but passing it will mean receiving the degree of "The Friend of God" and the diploma of "The Father of All Them That Believe" (Romans 4:11).

The supreme trial came clear and decisive. There could be no mistake. The voice announcing the staggering command was the voice he knew. It was the voice of his heavenly Friend. "Take now thy son, thine only son Isaac, whom thou lovest . . . and offer *him* . . ." (Genesis 22:2). But could he trust the voice of his heavenly Friend *now?* Now, when the next step seemed like sheer disaster? It seemed like a leap over the precipice. Reason might well have said: "God promised you this son. He was given you by God's power. All your hopes and expectations center in him. In him runs the line of the promised Redeemer. How can God demand that he be slain?"

Faith does not question God's Word. Faith asks no "Why?" concerning the divine will. Years of trusting had prepared God's valiant pilgrim for this supreme crisis. He had proved God and knew His faithfulness. But could he go through with this? Could he trust God supremely? Was God *really* first in his life?

III. OBEDIENCE IS THE TEST OF FAITH

1. *Faith Is Necessary to Obedience*. Abraham had the prerequisite faith to produce obedience. Therefore his response to the divine word was magnificent despite the fact that the command involved was staggering, and to the flesh at least unreasonable. There was not a moment's hesitation. No expression of complaint escaped his lips. No plea for excuse. No begging off. The only answer God's heroic warrior gave was that he rose up early and began the journey to lonely Moriah's brow with Isaac. He believed that God would either "provide himself a lamb for a burnt-offering" (Genesis 22:8) or, if not, would raise Isaac up, "even from the dead" (Hebrews 11:19). Faith became vocal when Abraham said to the two young men who accompanied him and Isaac: "Abide ye here . . . I and the lad will go yonder and worship, and *come again to you*" (Genesis 22:5).

2. *Faith Is Proved by Obedience*. The altar was prepared, the wood was laid in order, Isaac was bound, and Abraham raised the knife to slay his son. So far as God was concerned the act was completed. Abraham's faith was proved. God's voice reversed the order. "Lay not thine hand upon the lad . . . for now I know that thou fearest God . . ." (Genesis 22:12).

IV. GOD ALWAYS REWARDS OBEDIENCE

1. *God Rewards Obedience in This Life*. Isaac is spared, and in the bushes caught by his horns, Abraham sees a ram for the sacrifice. Instead of a place of unutterable woe and grief the spot is transformed into holy ground. Instead of "Thou Lord hast forgotten," the mount is called "Jehovah-Jireh," "Thou Lord, dost see!" What a precious thought! In our darkest hour of testing, in our dreariest moment of trial, we can confidently know, "Thou Lord, dost see! Thou Lord, dost care!" How comforting to know in such a moment that there is no temptation taken us but such as is common to man.

How unspeakably precious to prove that "God is faithful," who will not suffer us to be tempted above that we are able "but will with the temptation also make a way of escape" that we "may be able to bear it" (I Corinthians 10:13).

When the last cherished Isaac is laid on the altar and every idol is broken at the feet of Him who is "King of kings and Lord of lords," we too shall see heaven open and hear the voice of God sweeter than music of angelic choir: "By Myself have I sworn, saith the Lord, for because thou *hast done* this thing . . . that in blessing I will bless thee . . ." (Genesis 22:16, 17).

Now, to the heart of faith, the obedient heart, the yielded heart, He will give: Instead of dry land, springs of water! Instead of heaviness, the garment of praise! Instead of the thorn, the fig tree! Instead of the brier, the myrtle tree! Instead of ashes, beauty!

2. *God Will Reward Obedience in the Life to Come.* Now, in this life, we are enrolled in the school of faith. Now is the time for discipline and study. Now is the time for submission to the divine will. Now is the time to prepare for the final examination! Then graduation from time to eternity! Then we shall receive the diploma, "Well done, thou good and faithful servant: enter thou into the joy of thy Lord" (Matthew 25:21).

At the Judgment Seat of Christ faith and obedience will be tested and rewarded. Christian, what shall it be? Wood, hay and stubble to be burned up, or gold, silver and precious stones, to be purified and made finer to be laid at His blessed feet?

> O for a faith that will not shrink,
> Tho' pressed by ev'ry foe,
> That will not tremble on the brink
> Of any earthly woe!

That will not murmer or complain
  Beneath the chastening rod,
But, in the hour of grief or pain,
  Will lean upon its God.

A faith that shines more bright and clear
  When tempests rage without;
That when in danger knows no fear,
  In darkness feels no doubt.

—William H. Bathurst, 1831

Overcoming Fear

And he said unto them, Why are ye fearful? Have ye not yet faith (Mark 4:40).

TODAY, IN THE CLOSING YEARS of this dispensation, as faith is waning among the masses, fear is laying its crippling and paralyzing hand upon millions. "And there shall be signs in sun and moon and stars; and upon the earth distress of nations, in perplexity for the roaring of the sea and the billows; men fainting for fear, and for expectation of the things which are coming on the earth; for the powers of the heavens shall be shaken" (Luke 21:25, 26). Multitudes, who know not our Lord Jesus Christ and obey not His Gospel, are at a loss which way to turn. Many of God's own children are beset by doubts and uncertainties. Peace, security and happiness, so tenaciously striven after, so zealously sought for, seem to elude man's grasp and fail and fade like the mirage of the desert. The pall of night ever threatens to settle down upon the noontide of the world's flimsy happiness.

Is there no respite from this dread contagion of fear, no deliverance from the epidemic of uncertainty? For the believer there is, of course, release, full and complete, in God's gracious provision. But the world sunk in unbelief and sin can look for no relief. While the child of God must not expect to be immune from the temptations, dangers and commotions of this life, he can meet them victoriously, maintaining always the peace of God in his soul. He must not be under any illusion, however, that he will not run into dangers and storms in his journey through the world.

82

I. THE VOYAGE OF LIFE IS BESET WITH PERIL AND FEAR

This world, which sin has invaded, is like a Tiberian lake, sometimes tranquil and peaceful, its placid surface gilded with the setting sun, but easily angered, often unmanageably boisterous. The non-Christian must cross the sea of life without chart and compass and the presence of the Saviour on board. The true disciple of Christ has chart and compass and the presence of Christ with him in the voyage of life.

1. *Being a Christian, However, Does Not Shield from the Storm.* Not only so, but the pathway of true consecration and obedience to the Saviour often leads through troubled waters. "When even was come" it was the Saviour who said to the disciples, "Let us go over unto the other side." It was in obedience to His command that they left the shore to embark upon the quiet waters, as twilight slowly settled down. But soon His way, which by their obedience became their way, became stormy and tempestuous. "And there ariseth a great storm of wind, and the waves beat into the boat insomuch that the boat was now filled" (Mark 4:37).

Obeying Christ often involves suffering and persecution, as Christ suffered and was persecuted. "A servant is not greater than his lord. If they persecuted me, they will also persecute you . . ." (John 15:20). "Yea, and all that would live Godly in Christ Jesus shall suffer persecution" (II Timothy 3:12). The true disciple of Christ is subject to hatred and scorn from the world—often tacit, unexpressed, but easily discoverable when the test is applied. "If the world hateth you, ye know that it hath hated me before it hated you. If ye were of the world the world would love its own but because ye are not of the world, but I have chosen you out of the world, therefore the world hateth you" (John 15:18, 19).

2. *Being a Christian Enables One to Weather the Storm.* Sometimes the child of God runs head on into a terrific tempest. The winds howl and waves lash angrily. The little bark fills with water and Christ, Himself, is "in the stern,

asleep." It is then that fear is most likely to lay its iron grasp upon the believer's heart and to congeal it with its icy touch.

There are storms without, inevitable, unavoidable, certain as the stars in their courses. But more subtle and more dangerous are the storms within. But if we can rest serenely in the consciousness that an omnipotent Christ is with us in our frail boat, we can enjoy an inner poise that will keep us miraculously safe in the very vortex of the maelstrom without.

II. CHRIST ALONE CAN STILL OUR FEAR

The tempest into which the disciples ran was not an accident. The Saviour, who was asleep in the boat, knew it was going to occur. Christ's service does not exempt His servants from storms. The stoutest heart, the ablest seaman may well fear when the angry gale whips the waves into fury.

1. *Unbelief Produces Fear.* This was the source of the disciples' trouble. Unbelief took possession of them. Without implicit faith in Christ the bravest heart will falter. Because of the raging storm the disciples in a moment became as helpless as children. It did not take them long to see their utter impotence in the face of imminent death that threatened. It was then that fear laid hold upon them and they hastened to awaken Jesus.

"Teacher, carest thou not that we perish?" It was the voice of their unbelief accusing Him of unconcern for them and their safety. But, being Master of wind and wave, and Creator of the fathomless sea, could He be unconcerned about any danger arising from the storm either to Himself or to them? Had they known Him more intimately and trusted Him more implicitly, they might well have shared the splendid peace and poise He enjoyed. However, like many of the Lord's disciples the pressure of circumstances overcame them. They were filled with tension and strain. Before they were aware, they were reduced to that lamentable state of fearfulness and fretfulness, all too frequent among the professing followers of Christ. They began to doubt and to complain against the Lord Himself, and to question His care for them.

2. *Faith Dissipates Fear.* Believing God is the panacea for every inward disturbance. We would be in a happy condition indeed if we never doubted God or never questioned His care or concern for us. How much worry and anxiety we would spare ourselves! What quietness and confidence would be ours even though the sea about us might be lashed into fury and the snarling waves break into our frail craft. But the Master of the sea and the Lord of creation knows our human frailty. Though He may seem to be asleep in the hinder part of the boat and oblivious to our peril, yet when the furious tempest is upon us and the swirling waves threaten to engulf us, when we call upon Him He will arise for our help and we may say with the Psalmist:

> "My help cometh from Jehovah
> Who made heaven and earth.
> He will not suffer thy foot to be moved:
> He that keepeth thee will not slumber.
> Behold, He that keepeth Israel
> Will neither slumber nor sleep" (Psalm 121:2-4).

"He that keepeth thee will not slumber!" Can we, dare we, believe that this is true *always* — under all trials and tribulations, in every circumstance and condition of life? Sometimes, when we cannot, and the situation appears hopeless, and we struggle vainly in the fury of the tempest, He, the infinitely gracious One, nevertheless will still the storm, which no one else but He can calm. "And he awoke, and rebuked the wind, and said unto the sea, Peace, be still. And the wind ceased, and there was a great calm" (Mark 4:39). Those who look to Him in times of trouble and commotion and unfalteringly trust Him experience the "great calm."

III. *Learning to Know Christ Is the Secret of Removing Our Fear*

We need not fear the storm if we know Him who can still

the storm. In proportion as we know Him and trust Him will we be delivered from the unrest and commotion of the world about us and be able to maintain inner calm and quiet of soul. "He is our peace" (Ephesians 2:14). Knowing Him is the only true pathway to peace.

1. *The Occasion of Fear Often Presents Christ.* He who is "our refuge and strength, a very present help in time of trouble" (Psalm 46:1) graciously manifests Himself in times of distress. Frequently the storm is providentially permitted to cause us to know Him better. It was so with the distraught disciples on the Sea of Galilee. When the tumultuous elements subsided and calm once again settled down upon the scene, the value of the event to the twelve is revealed in their question, "Who then is this, that even the wind and the sea obey Him?" (Mark 4:41).

2. *The Occasion of Fear Often Provokes Earnest Inquiry After Christ.* "Who then is this?" It was an exceedingly important question, worth all the danger and discomfort of the tempest that prompted it. Any experience, however discomforting and trying, is worthwhile if it makes us enquire more diligently after Christ. In the storm, but particularly in the calm that followed, they saw something new and revealing in Jesus they had never seen before, although they had been with Him for some time now.

They had seen Him in many circumstances. They had heard many different tones in that voice, which was always pure melody. But now as He stood there in the boat, majestically quieting the turbulent sea with greater ease than a mother soothes her fretful babe to sleep, they discovered in their Master new beauty and excellence of character and hitherto undisclosed power and authority of person demanding a more intensive discipleship. "Who then is this?" It is as though they said: "We must get nearer to Him! We must get to know Him better!"

Could anyone be conducted to a finer attitude of soul

than that to which the disciples were led by the storm? Down
through the centuries God has brought countless others to a
similar blessed attitude of heart through storms. Tempest-
tossed voyagers, filled with dread and uncertainty, have heard
His voice speaking in love and compassion amid the winds
and waves and the sudden calm, "Why are ye fearful? *Have
ye not yet faith?*" It is *faith* that removes our fears because
faith enables us to know Him better, who is the source of all
calm.

Almost two thousand years have passed, and though we
know more in some ways than these men, yet in times of
strain and stress we are still driven to say, "Who then is
this?" In the answer to that question lies the secret of rest
and deliverance from fear. In the degree that we really know
Him, in that degree shall we be fearless and quiet amid all
the commotions of life. In proportion as we become acquainted with Him through trusting Him shall we experience
the peace of God, which passeth all understanding, guarding
our hearts and our thoughts in Christ Jesus.

> Bringing life, and health and gladness,
>   All around this heav'nly Guest,
> Banished unbelief and sadness,
>   Changed our weariness to rest.
>
> What a wonderful salvation,
>   Where we always see His face;
> What a perfect habitation,
>   What a quiet resting place.
>
> Blessed quietness, holy quietness,
>   What assurance in my soul!
> On the stormy sea,
> He speaks peace to me
>   How the billows cease to roll!
>   —*Manie Payne Ferguson*

Living By Faith in the Son of God

> *I have been crucified with Christ; and it is no longer I that live, but Christ liveth in me and that life which I now live in the flesh I live in faith, the faith which is in the Son of God, who loved me, and gave himself up for me* (Galatians 2:20 R. V.).

THE APOSTLE PAUL was just as sure that he was living the Christian life by faith as he was that he had begun the Christian life by faith. If we are to live the Christian life as it ought to be lived, we must be equally certain that the life we now live in the flesh we "live in faith, that faith which is in the Son of God," who loved us and gave Himself up for us (Galatians 2:20). Yet faith in the Son of God, which brings victory and blessing into Christian living, is all too rare among the people of God. Is there any other way to live the Christian life than by faith? If our own puny efforts and contaminated works are unable to save us, can they possibly be of any more avail to help us live a life acceptable and well-pleasing to God? Certainly not. It is just as impossible to live the Christian life acceptably on any other basis than faith as it is to begin the Christian life on any other principle. Christian living is made possible by faith, and by faith alone.

Out of whose innermost being are the "rivers of living water" to flow? Out of him who strives, works and struggles? Nay. "He that *believeth* on me, as the scripture hath said, out of his . . . innermost being shall flow rivers of living water" (John 7:38). But are we not to rely upon ourselves, our strength, our will power, our human morality and ethics? Nay, says the apostle. "The life which I now live in the flesh I live in faith, the faith which is in the Son of God,"

I. FAITH IN THE SON OF GOD FURNISHES THE KEY OF ACCESS
TO FULLNESS OF LIFE

Do you stand amidst grief and disappointment? Are you
hedged in and hindered on every hand by defeat and failure?
Is your Christian experience joyless and unvictorious? Do you
stand as it were with Martha of old at the grave of Lazarus,
hopeless and helpless? Can you not hear the Saviour, who
conquered sin and death for you, calling across the centuries
to triumph in His triumph, to rejoice in His victory? "Said I
not unto thee, that, if thou wouldest believe, thou shouldest
see the glory of God?" (John 11:40). Would you see the
glory of God? Would you unlock the mystic treasures of that
resplendent truth, "Christ in you, the hope of glory" (Colossians 1:27)? Would you strike the inexhaustible spring
that will flow out into a river of blessing? The *key is faith*.
You must believe. You must believe on Christ "as the
scripture hath said."

Why the great disparity between what we are in Christ,
and what we claim and appropriate as our possessions here
and now? The answer: We refuse to *believe* God's Word!
We refuse to *believe we are what we are in Christ and to
act upon that position!* We hesitate to go up and possess the
land of spiritual conquest. We refuse to possess our possessions
in Christ. If ever the benefits Christ purchased for me are to
be enjoyed here and now, I must believe they are mine, and
take them as mine. I must believe in my identification with
Christ in death and resurrection. I must believe apart from
my feelings, fears, struggles, failures and confusion—the old
way of self and the flesh. I must count on Him!

Grasping what our position in Christ really means, and by
faith appropriating what our participation in Christ implies,
will be a gateway to a whole unexplored continent of spiritual
privilege and power, a portal to such happiness as we never
dreamed possible this side of heaven. Faith furnishes the key
of access. But what must I believe?

1. *I Must Believe That Christ Died for Me.* "Christ died for our sins according to the scriptures" (I Corinthians 15:3). First and foremost for my welfare this is what the scripture hath said concerning Christ. He died for *me!* He bore *my* sins "in his own body on the tree" (I Peter 2:24). He justifies me freely "by his grace through the redemption that is in Christ Jesus" (Romans 3:24). God is declared to be "just, and the justifier of him who believeth in Jesus" (Romans 3:26). Believing this testimony of God concerning His Son, I have access into eternal life.

2. *I Must Believe That I Died in Christ.* I must believe that when I trusted Christ as my Saviour, I believed "into Him." "He that believeth . . . on Him (into vital union with Him) as the scripture hath said" (John 7:38) shall have the rivers of blessing welling up in his heart. Saving faith is believing into Christ — a state of vital union with Him and all other believers in Him. It is not a mere intellectual belief in a historical Christ. It is not merely believing that Christ *died,* but that He died *for me,* and that I died *in Him.* When He died, I died! "God so loved the world, that he gave his only begotten Son that whosoever believeth . . . on [*into*] *Him* should not perish, but have everlasting life" (John 3:16). "He that believeth *into Him* is not condemned" (verse 18), but he "that believeth not is condemned already, because he hath not *believed into the name* of the only begotten Son of God" (original translation from Greek).

3. *I Must Believe That I Arose in Christ.* Believing into a position of vital union with Him, we become one with Him not only in death, but in resurrection as well. The new creation is life in union with Christ Jesus. If the Head shares life, shall not the body also? Our positional death to sin and self and to all that we were in fallen Adam, is the gateway to a larger, fuller life in Christ. Having signed the death warrant to the "old life" and having consigned it to the grace, for we are sharers of Christ's tomb (Romans 6:4),

we discover that we are recipients of a life infinitely more wonderful — the life of the ages. "God, who is rich in mercy, for his great love wherewith he loved us. . . hath quickened us together with Christ . . . and . . . *raised us up together*" (Ephesians 2:5, 6).

Christ's resurrection *my* resurrection! God hath raised me up together with Him. Here is something for my deepest need! Life! Power! Blessing! This exceeding greatness of His power becomes available "to us-ward who believe, according to the working of his mighty power, which he wrought in Christ, when he raised him from the dead" (Ephesians 1:19, 20).

4. *I Must Believe That As I Reckon on My Position in Christ Its Benefits Becomes Experimentally Real.* What a vast difference there often is between our unchanging position in Christ and our changeable practice in life, between our glorious standing and our too-often inglorious state. We are princes, but we frequently act like slaves. We are wealthy, but live as beggars. We are clothed in linen clean and white, but live as though covered with rags. We have manna from heaven, but eat the weak and beggarly elements of the world. We have water of life from the rock, but languish with thirst in the desert. We have the pillar of cloud by day and the pillar of fire by night, but stumble on in our own folly and self-sufficiency.

II. FAITH IN THE SON OF GOD DETERMINES THE DEGREE TO WHICH WE ENJOY FULLNESS OF LIFE

The Word of God through Isaiah to the faithless Ahaz may well be applied to every believer, hesitating and wavering on the threshold of spiritual conquest and blessing: "If ye will not believe, surely ye shall not be established" (Isaiah 7:9).

1. *Believing That Christ Died for Me Brings Me Life.* I receive a new nature. The Holy Spirit comes into my

heart to dwell. Eternal death, the penalty of sin, is removed. I am baptized spiritually into Christ, His body the Church, and become vitally one with all true believers. I am sealed with the Holy Spirit and stamped as God's own until the day of redemption. Positionally, I am perfect in Christ, one with Him for all eternity — a son, a priest and heir.

Why, then, you say, are there defeat, disappointment and struggle? Why so little experimental realization of what I am in Christ? The answer: There is life, and there is fullness of life; there is the indwelling of the Spirit, and there is the fullness of the Spirit. As your faith, so be it unto you. You are a child of God: will you believe it, and thus enjoy the freedom of a son? You have the privilege of being filled with the Spirit: will you believe that God will fill you? You died with Christ: will you believe that you are dead to sin and self? You arose with Him: will you appropriate His resurrection power?

2. *Believing That I Died in Christ Brings Me Fullness of Life.* Life is not enough. I need fullness of life. The little streamlet will not suffice. Jesus promised, and I need, rivers of living water. It is not enough that I go to heaven myself. I must become a channel of victory and blessing that others through me may find the heavenly way. Realizing that I died *in* Christ is just as important a part of the Gospel as that Christ died *for* me. Both aspects of the Cross are the Gospel. Let us not separate in our thinking and living what God has joined together.

The requirements of the New Testament as they bear upon the Christian life all presuppose this oneness of the believer with Christ in the power of His resurrection. Everywhere the Christian life is placed in the realm of human impossibility. A supernatural standard is set. The Christian life is placed on the plane of the miraculous. He who would live it must cease to move in the realm of the purely natural. Like Peter we essay to walk on the waves. We dare not look at the billows or listen to the boisterous winds. The moment we do, we sink, and hear the warning words of the Saviour, "O thou of little faith, wherefore didst thou doubt?" (Matthew 14:31). But looking to Jesus, and to Him alone, the miracle occurs. The waters become firm to support our assured step. The step lengthens into a walk. The walk merges into a life—a life the testimony of which becomes that of the great apostle: "I have been crucified with Christ; and it is no longer I that live, but Christ liveth in me: and that life which I now live in the flesh I live in faith, the faith which is in the Son of God, who loved me, and gave himself up for me" (Galatians 2:20 R.V.).

> This is my wonderful story,
>   Christ to my heart has come;
> Jesus, the King of Glory,
>   Finds in my heart a home.
>
> Now in His bosom confiding,
>   This my glad song shall be;
> I am in Jesus abiding,
>   Jesus abides in me.
>
> Christ in me, Christ in me,
>   Christ in me, wonderful story,
> Christ in me, Christ in me,
>   Christ in me, hope of glory.
>
>   —*A. B. Simpson*

To which we may add the glorious concomitant truth:

> I in Christ, I in Christ,
>   I in Christ, wonderful story,
> I in Christ, I in Christ,
>   I in Christ, hope of glory.

Triumphing in Christ

And having spoiled principalities and powers, he made a show of them openly, triumphing over them in it (Colossians 2:15). But thanks be unto God, who always leadeth us in triumph in Christ . . . (II Corinthians 2:14).

THE SINISTER FACT of the existence of evil in the world is everywhere apparent. On every hand we see countless proofs that evil forces are ceaselessly at work in innumerable ways and through many channels. Obvious everywhere is an aggressive opposition to God and God's purpose. It is apparent, too, that this evil is not a mere abstraction. Behind the evil manifested in human personality there is a supernatural personality, Satan, and an organized kingdom of helpers called demons.

Alongside of the fact of the existence of evil is the fact of good in the world. Good forces are also at work. There is a good power working for the regeneration of mankind and the glory of God. There is observable in the universe an aggressive opposition to Satan and Satan's purpose. Moreover, good is no more an abstraction than evil. It is the product of personality. One is good and that One is God (Luke 18:19). The evil one is the opposite of the Good One, and Scripture presents Satan as the great antagonist of God and man.

The existence of evil and good in the world leads to a third fact so clearly observable all about us, namely, the fact of conflict in the world. On the threshold of revelation we read the far-reaching prophecy of a clash between God and

Satan. "And I will put hostility between thee and the woman, and between thy seed and her seed; and he shall bruise thy head, and thou shalt bruise his heel" (Genesis 3:15). Every page of the Bible is a record of this dramatic and terrific struggle, and an unfolding of its progress toward its divinely ordained end — the ultimate and absolute defeat of Satan and the eternal perfect victory of God.

This situation inevitably leads to a fourth inescapable fact: namely, *our* conflict. It is impossible for us to decide for God's cause, to cast our lot in God's camp, become identified with our Lord Jesus Christ by faith, and escape war. Christ's struggle against the evil one becomes our struggle. Christ's temptations become our temptations. As He was, so are we in this world (I John 4:17). If we go forth without the camp bearing His reproach, if we grow in grace and launch out into the deep things of God, we shall frequently come into direct clash with the devil. If with unfaltering faith we reckon upon our oneness with our divine Lord, we shall know first hand what it is to "wrestle against principalities and powers" against "rulers of this darkness," against "wicked spirits in the heavenlies" (Ephesians 6:12). In a most definite and inescapable way, as we count upon our union with our Lord, we shall find *His* conflict becomes *our* conflict. What, then, is Christ's conflict?

I. CHRIST'S CONFLICT IS THE STRUGGLE OF GOD AGAINST SATAN — GOOD AGAINST EVIL

1. *The Commencement of the Struggle Is to Be Traced in the Past.* When the world was young, when the "morning stars sang together and the sons of God shouted for joy" (Job 38:7), when not a cloud bedimmed God's sinless creation, when all God's angels reposed in virgin purity, and the vast spheres were keyed to one unbroken paean of praise and glory to God, before man was created, *sin began!* A dark cloud arose to bedim the glory of the sinless spheres. In the heart of one

of the highest of God's sinless creatures sin was born. The "Anointed Cherub," who protected the very throne of God, stood up. In a loud harsh voice that for the first time disturbed the majestic and mighty harmony of the sinless creation he cried in vaulting pride and ambition:

> I will ascend into heaven
> I will exalt my throne above the stars of God
> I will sit also upon the mountain of the congregation . . .
> I will ascend above the clouds
> I will be like the Most High!" (Isaiah 14:13, 14).

Treason and anarchy had invaded the universe. Pride and presumption made an archangel an archdevil. Self-will hurled against the divine will commenced the deadly conflict. Sin and self began their long march of blood and tears.

2. *The Consequence of the Struggle Must Be Faced in the Present.* The archenemy not only led a vast revolt among the angelic beings, but deceived and enslaved the human race through our first parents. God's infinite grace initiated the glorious plan of redemption through Christ. Satan thought he had won the first round in the battle. Genesis 3:15 was God's declaration of war against the despoiler and the announcement of the divine plan for the redemption and restoration of the human race and the re-establishment of God's undivided sovereignty over the world.

The finished work of Christ on the Cross provided a way of escape for all who had fallen under the power of sin and Satan. Man fell under the sway of Satan's kingdom and under the dominion of Satan's kingship (Matthew 12:26; John 8:44). By faith in Christ man is "delivered from the power of darkness" and "translated" into "the kingdom of God's dear Son" (Colossians 1:13). Without God's remedy man faces the penalty of sin, which is eternal death (John 3:16-18), and lies at the mercy of Satan, ruined and enslaved.

When a soul trusts Christ, he is delivered from the penalty of sin. As a Christian he must face the question of the power of sin. As he reckons upon his glorious position in Christ (Romans 6:11), and realizes in a Spirit-filled walk his birthright of victory over sin, he faces subtle and fierce temptation and attack from the evil one (Ephesians 6:10-20). Only as he realizes his victory in the Victorious One can the believer overcome the forces that oppose him.

Thus both the unbeliever and the believer must face the results of the fall of man and the presence of deadly conflict in the world, the former as a slave, shackled and fettered under sentence of doom, the latter as a freedman, with the sentence of doom forever remitted, but who is confronted with the constant danger of being tempted and fettered so that his testimony and service will be effectually hindered or destroyed altogether.

3. *The Consummation of the Struggle Is to Be Placed in the Future.* Concerning its final outcome, the Scriptures express the most absolute and undeviating certainty. Christ is to be completely and triumphantly victorious. On the Cross He "spoiled principalities and powers," disarming them, making a show of them openly (Colossians 2:15). He arose from death, ascended far above all principality and power to God's right hand, where He waits until "His enemies are made the footstool of his feet" (Psalm 110:1; Hebrews 2:14). At His glorious Second Advent Satan will be bound, the kingdom set up (Revelation 20:1-3). After the Kingdom Age, there will be a short manifestation of Satanic power after he is loosed, but then he is cast forever into the Lake of Fire (Revelation 20:10), and for eternity God will be all in all (I Corinthians 15:24-28), with every enemy forever put down.

II. CHRIST'S CONFLICT BECOMES OUR CONFLICT

I. *The Conflict Is the Result of Our Identification with Christ.* Believing in Christ means being baptized by the Holy Spirit into vital spiritual union with Him, as the children of Israel were "baptized into Moses in the cloud and in the sea" (I Corinthians 10:2). Just as the ancient people of

God were cut off from Egypt and Pharaoh's oppression by the Red Sea, and came under a new leader so when we are regenerated, we are simultaneously baptized by the Spirit "into Christ," into His death, burial and resurrection (Romans 6:3, 4). Thus becoming one with the Son of God by position, we come under the same hatred and attack to which He was subjected from Satan. His conflict becomes our conflict because we become *one* in *life* and *destiny* with Him.

2. *The Conflict Is in Proportion As We Reckon upon Our Identification with Christ.* As we by faith translate our position of oneness in Christ into an experimentally realized possession (Romans 6:1-11), we shall find the Saviour's love for sinners, His devotion to the Father's will and His passion for the Father's glory, burning in our souls. But not only so, we shall begin to experience something of the intensity of conflict that faced the Saviour — those lonely hours of temptation in the desert, the intense opposition of sinners, Gethsemane's dark shadows, and Calvary's agony. It is reckoning upon our union with Christ that brings the intensified struggle against the kingdom of Satan. What a terrific battle! What manifold temptation! What severe testings! Relentlessly there will be the flash of sharp steel, the piercing battle cry, the fierce onslaught.

But is this all? No. Thank God we may turn to a brighter side. After the noise of battle has died away, after the enemy has fallen slain upon the field, or fled in turmoil from the fray, we may take rich spoil and rejoice in victory.

III. CHRIST'S TRIUMPH BECOMES OUR TRIUMPH

1. *Our Triumph Is Assured in Him!* The Apostle Paul knew the intense conflict. He also experienced the triumph. Being delivered out of great peril at Ephesus and out of deep and painful anxiety concerning the church at Corinth, the dauntless warrior of Christ could cry: "Thanks be unto God, who always causes us to have a triumph in Christ"

(II Corinthians 2:14). He was using a bold figure and capturing the splendor and pomp of one of the greatest of all Roman scenes and pageants — an imperial triumph! In his mind's eye he saw the Roman general arrayed in silken garments, riding regally in his chariots at the head of his victorious legions. The apostle saw the princes and potentates, who had been taken captive, walking in chains beside the wheels of the conqueror's chariot. He visualized the long and magnificent procession moving along the Appian Way or along the Via Sacra, while clouds of incense ascended to heaven from the altars, which had been set up along the line of march. It was the acme of triumph.

But Paul used the figure taken from contemporary Roman life of a far greater triumph — his triumph in Christ. Not as the climax of some great campaign in distant lands, not as the crowning event of a life-long military career, but continually, in the midst of his battles and testings, in the midst of seeming defeats, Christ was always leading him in triumph! That continual triumph *can* be ours! It *ought* to be ours! By His grace it *must* be ours. Shall we by faith take it and make it ours, as did the apostle?

2. *Our Triumph Is Realized by Faith.* Like Paul we face the far greater triumph. It is the triumph of the Christian who believes in and acts upon his vital union with the Son of God. Will we dare to *believe* we are *what we are* in Christ? Will we use the key of faith to open the door to victory and blessing? Will we dare to convert our perfect position in Christ into a worthy practice?

By faith we, too, can triumph as they triumphed. Realizing we are what we are in Christ and counting upon the privileges and potentialities of that position in Him who "spoiled principalities and powers" and who "made a show of them openly, triumphing over them in it," we, too, can shout with Paul: "But thanks be unto God, who always leadeth us in triumph in Christ!" God grant us that faith and give us the shout!

> His banner over us is love,
>   Our sword the Word of God;
> We tread the road the saints above
>   With shouts of triumph trod.
> By faith they, like a whirlwind's breath,
>   Swept on o'er every field;
> The faith by which they conquered death
>   Is still our shining shield.
>
> Faith is the victory!
> Faith is the victory!
> Faith is the victory!
> That overcomes the world.
>   —*John H. Yates*

CHAPTER FOUR

THE PATHWAY OF CONSECRATION

Giving Ourselves to the Lord

They . . . first gave their own selves to the Lord . . .
(II Corinthians 8:5).

THE DEDICATION OF ONE'S SELF to God is possible only for the Christian, but it is the supreme duty and privilege of *every* Christian. Never must becoming a Christian through the act of accepting Christ as personal Saviour, resulting in forgiveness of sins and regeneration, be confused with the act of yielding the redeemed life entirely to God. In the case of perhaps a few Christians the acceptance of Christ as Saviour and the presentation of the life to Him for service occur simultaneously. But in the vast majority of instances conversion to God precedes the dedication of the life to Him by a period of time, sometimes extending over many years.

Dedication or the yielding of the regenerated life to God begins with a crisis involving a specific decision and act. Its development, on the other hand, is dependent upon the maintenance of the attitude of yieldedness in the believer's life. In short, the yielded life is a once-for-all submitting of the whole being to God to use as He sees fit, but it also involves a life-time working out of the details of the initial unreserved surrender.

The believer either has or has not made the initial complete surrender. If he has not, his life may be yielded to God to a degree, but not entirely. If he has, he may be living up to the terms of his contract with God, and thus enjoying a life of entire yieldedness to God's will, or he may not be continuously yielding. In the latter case he must return to the terms of his original agreement to be restored to full blessing.

The Macedonian Christians experienced the blessings of the yielded life. They not only knew the joy of giving, but experienced the supreme joy of giving the greatest gift the believer can give God — *the gift of himself*. "They . . . first gave *their own selves* to the Lord." Their giving, moreover, was in the proper order. "They *first* gave their own selves to the Lord." It was natural that they experienced fulness of joy in all their subsequent giving, because when we give ourselves unto the Lord, we give Him all we have, to be called for, and disposed of, according to His will.

Little wonder then we read of these noble consecrated saints: "How that in a great trial of affliction the abundance of their joy and their deep poverty abounded unto the riches of their liberality" (II Corinthians 8:2). What a combination! Affliction and joy! Deep poverty and abounding liberality! It is an impossible union except when we are entirely dedicated to Christ, as they were.

I. EVERY CHRISTIAN SHOULD GIVE HIMSELF TO THE LORD

Many Christians balk at the idea of consecration and ask by life if not by lip, "Why should I give myself to the Lord?" They do not see the yielded life as the definite duty or the specific responsibility of every believer, or what is a thousand-fold more blessed, as a glorious privilege which God has bestowed upon us — the honor of presenting ourselves "a living sacrifice" unto Him (Romans 12:1). Yet the most cogent reasons exist why every Christian should unreservedly give himself to God.

1. *We Should Give Ourselves to the Lord Because the Lord Gave Himself for Us.* "God so loved the world that he gave his only begotten Son" for us (John 3:16). The Father gave heaven's best to provide salvation for us. "He spared not his own Son, but delivered him up for us all" (Romans 8:32).

The Son gave up the glory which He had with the Father "before the world was" (John 17:5) for us. Our Lord suffered in the garden and was crucified on Golgotha's brow for us. Behold His love and His mercies for us.

Paul was thinking of the love of God manifested in our Lord's giving Himself for us as a motive for our giving ourselves to Him when he wrote to the Christians at Rome: "I beseech you therefore, brethren, by the *mercies of God,* that ye present your bodies a living sacrifice, holy, acceptable unto God, which is your reasonable service" (Romans 12:1). And what could be more "reasonable" in the light of the wonderful love exhibited in our Lord's giving Himself for us than that we in turn should gladly and spontaneously give ourselves unto Him?

God graciously speaks of our presenting our bodies to Him as a "sacrifice," but when we catch a glimpse of that immeasurable work which Jesus our Lord wrought for us on the Cross, we blush with shame to call our yieldedness a sacrifice. Rather we are aroused to the realization that to be allowed to present our lives into the service of such a Lord and Master is an *honor* greater than human heart can understand or human tongue describe.

2. *We Should Give Ourselves to the Lord Because We Are Not Our Own, We Belong to Him.* All men belong to God by virtue of creation. But through the fall humanity has been taken over by Satan and alienated from God. By redemption the believer is not only bought back and brought back to God, but he becomes God's property in a most real and vital sense. The Apostle Paul had in mind God's peculiar ownership of His redeemed children when he wrote to the Corinthians: "What? know ye not that your body is the temple of the Holy Spirit, who is in you, whom ye have of God, and *ye are not your own,* for ye are bought with a price: therefore glorify God in your body . . ." (I Corinthians 6:19, 20).

There is no more powerful incentive to full consecration to God, next to realizing the divine love in our Lord's giving Himself for us, than to understand the claim God has upon our bodies, our talents, our strength, our time, and all that we are. To act upon this truth in surrendering ourselves completely to Him who redeemed us is the gateway to the inflow of God's power and blessing into our lives.

3. *We Should Give Ourselves to the Lord Because We Shall Never Fully Enjoy the Christian Life Until We Do So.* The world's glitter will dazzle us, its pleasures and pursuits will allure us, its temptations and trials will overcome us until we yield completely to Christ. If we would have Him become "the lily of the valley," "the rose of Sharon," "the fairest of ten thousand," the One altogether lovely to the soul, we must dedicate all to Him. When we open life's greatest treasure of ourselves to God, God's greatest treasure of Himself shall be manifested in and through us.

II. EVERY CHRISTIAN SHOULD GIVE HIMSELF TO THE LORD IN A MANNER APPROPRIATE TO THE PRIVILEGE

It is unthinkable that our giving should be half-hearted and partial, or rendered with a grudging spirit, or offered with reservations, or performed fearfully and with misgivings. It is impossible, moreover, that we could offer some substitute for ourselves. Never must we be deceived into imagining that our strength, time, labor, or money can ever make up for our refusal to give ourselves.

It must always be remembered that our Lord does not so much want that which is ours, but *us!* If He has us, He has all that is ours and more. When the noble Macedonians "*first* gave their own selves to the Lord," they naturally gave bountifully of their means, so much so that they besought the apostle and his colleagues with much intreaty that they would receive their gifts for the poor (II Corinthians 8:4-6).

1. *We Must Give Ourselves Unto the Lord Willingly.*

Considering it as a high honor and a sacred privilege, rather than a stern duty, and resting on the wondrous love manifested at Calvary, our yielding must be voluntary and never mandatory. True love is never coerced. It is wooed and won. Hence the language of God's love is "I *beseech* you therefore, brethren, by the mercies of God, that ye present your bodies a living sacrifice." Surrender, which is not the result of our own free will but rendered grudgingly is no surrender at all.

2. *We Must Give Ourselves Unto the Lord Unconditionally.* There must be no reservations. Nothing must be held back. There can be no "ifs" in the contract. The gift of ourselves involves all we are or will be. Our Lord asks for the heart and the life. We must turn over the key to every room and every nook of the house in which we reside. He must have complete possession. We must yield a whole heart and life to receive the full blessing of a Risen Christ.

3. *We Must Give Ourselves Unto the Lord Trustingly.* How many believers are appalled by fears and misgivings when confronted with the challenge of full surrender. They react as if they were being asked to plunge over a precipice or place their lives in the hands of some dread foe or tyrant. But when we consider that we are committing ourselves to the supreme Friend and the infinitely loving Saviour of sinners, such an attitude betrays the most miserable unbelief.

If we cannot trust the Lord Jesus who died for us, whom, then, can we trust? If we cannot confidently put our lives in the hands of Him who made us, and remade us when broken by sin, in whose hands can we place ourselves? The redeemed soul has every reason to rest its case wholly and with calm assurance in the hands of the Son of God, both for time and eternity.

III. EVERY CHRISTIAN SHOULD ENJOY THE BLESSINGS RESULTING FROM GIVING HIMSELF TO THE LORD

Many of the Lord's people are satisfied with the enjoyment of so little of their heritage in Christ. They are content with a streamlet of refreshment when they might have "rivers of living water" flowing out of their innermost being (John 7:37-39). Like children they are wading in the shallows along the shoreline of the illimitable ocean of God's power when all the while the Holy Spirit is calling them to yield completely to God and launch out into the deep.

1. *We Should Enjoy the Blessings of God's Fulness.* No matter how filled with other things men's lives may be, they are empty if not filled with God. And God is waiting to fill our lives with His presence, if we give ourselves fully to Him. He is waiting to fill us with the Holy Spirit, with love, joy, peace, longsuffering, gentleness, goodness, faith, meekness and temperance. He is longing to fill us with power and victory. When the wicket gate of consecration is open, God's fulness will flow into the life as the waters fill the locks of a great canal when the sluices are opened.

The redeemed soul can experience no greater satisfaction or more genuine delight than God's manifested presence. Those who find the center of the divine will and the fulness of the divine presence, find the acme of bliss. Giving ourselves to the Lord will mean that our Lord will give Himself to us in full manifestation. Only then will our hearts well up in highest worship and adoration. Only then shall we be able to know the full blessing of God ourselves and be a medium of its communication to others. Only as we give ourselves to God can we bring the greatest glory to God, the greatest benefit to our fellowman and the greatest good to ourselves.

2. *We Should Enjoy the Blessing of the Widest Usefulness.* When our experience becomes Christ instead of self, holiness instead of worldliness, God instead of gold, separation instead of compromise with evil, we shall find that "a great door and effectual is opened" unto us for testimony and service (I Corinthians 16:9), and that God will cause us to triumph over the "many adversaries" that will be arrayed against our entering it. "Behold I have set before thee an open

door and no man can shut it" (Revelation 3:8) is the word of divine assurance to the yielded believer.

When our hearts and wills become one with God and we become fully aware that we are "workers together with him" (II Corinthians 6:1), busy about the same work He is engaged in, having the same aim as He has, then He can lavish His power upon us with the confidence we shall not dissipate it or prostitute it for selfish ends. Then we shall know the thrilling satisfaction of being used by God to glorify Him and to bring blessing and salvation to men.

So cogent are the reasons why the believer should give himself to the Lord and so great are the benefits resulting from the performance of this sacred duty and the acceptance of this sublime privilege that no believer dare hold back from yielding himself fully to Him who loved him and redeemed him with His own blood. God forbid that it should be said of any of us, as it was said of ancient Israel in the wilderness; "they could not enter in because of unbelief" (Hebrews 3:19).

The land is before us, "and surely it floweth with milk and honey" (Numbers 13:27). "Let us go up at once, and possess it; for we are well able to overcome it" (Numbers 13:30).

> O Jesus, Lord and Saviour,
>   I give myself to Thee,
> For Thou, in Thy atonement,
>   Didst give Thyself for me;
> I own no other Master,
>   My heart shall be Thy throne,
>   My life I give,
>   Henceforth to live,
>   O Christ, for Thee alone.
>   —*Thomas O. Chisholm*

Accepting God's Plan for Our Lives

For we are his workmanship, created in Christ Jesus unto good works, which God hath before ordained that we should walk in them (Ephesians 2:10).

WHEREVER WE LOOK in the universe we survey the glories of God's handiwork and the unmistakable evidences of His plan and purpose in all His mighty and manifold creation. The great Architect of the universe has plan and purpose in the sun and moon and each glittering orb in the starry vault of heaven. These heavenly bodies not only adorn the sky above but illuminate the earth beneath, and their courses are mapped out with minute and unerring accuracy.

The Creator of the worlds has plan and purpose in the turbulent mountain stream splashing over precipitous rocks, in the thundering cataract roaring majestically in its mighty power, in the illimitable ocean to which He has said, "Hitherto shalt thou come, but no further: and here shall thy proud waves be stayed" (Job 38:11). He has plan and purpose in the tiny flower that is "born to blush unseen and waste its fragrance on the desert air," in the smallest insect that crawls upon the earth, in the lumbering beast that tramps the tropical jungle. He has plan and purpose in each grain of sand in the trackless wastes of the scorching Sahara, in each rainbow tinted crystal of ice in the frozen fatnesses of the northland.

Everywhere we look in the physical sphere and in the lower creation we discover that God has plan and purpose for everything. Should we not find this fact abundantly more true in the life of man, who is the crown and goal of all creation and pre-eminently true in redeemed man restored in God's image and retrieved for God's service?

Has God given heaven's best to redeem us with no thought or end in view? Did Christ suffer and die with no purpose for his redeemed children? Are we saved merely to continue to live a self-planned life? Surely not. Such a conclusion would not only be contrary to reason but to the clear revelation of the Scriptures themselves.

I. God Has a Definite Plan for the Life of Every Child of His

This encouraging truth shines like a gem on the pages of Holy Scripture and compelling reasons are indicated why God has such a plan or purpose for the life of every child of His.

1. *God Has a Definite Plan for the Life of Every Child of His Because We Are His Creation.* He, the infinite Creator, "made us and not we ourselves, we are his people, and the sheep of his pasture" (Psalm 100:3). He, the almighty Potter, "formed man of the dust of the ground, and breathed into his nostrils the breath of life; and man became a living soul" (Genesis 2:7). He possessed our reins: He covered us in our "mother's womb." We can say with the Psalmist: "I will praise thee; for I am fearfully and wonderfully made: marvellous are thy works; and that my soul knoweth right well. My substance was not hid from thee, when I was made in secret, and curiously wrought in the lowest parts of the earth. Thine eye did see my substance, yet being imperfect; and in thy book all my members were written, which in continuance were fashioned, when as yet there was none of them. How precious are thy thoughts unto me, O God! how great is the sum of them. If I should count them, they are more in

number than the sand: when I awake, I am still with thee"
(Psalm 139:13-18).

2. *God Has a Definite Plan for the Life of Every Child
of His Because We Are His New Creation in Christ Jesus.*
Although the Creator took the dust of the ground and formed
and shaped it into an exquisite product of His skill called
"man," the product of His creative wisdom was soon marred.
Through Adam's fall sin wrecked God's handiwork. Through
the first man, the representative of the race, sin passed upon
the whole human family, so that the Apostle Paul declared,
"All have sinned" (Romans 3:23). "By one man sin entered
into the world, and death by sin; and so death passed upon
all men, for that all have sinned" (Romans 5:12). The
psalmist, conscious of his depravity and that of the whole race,
cried out lamentingly: "Behold, I was shapen in iniquity;
and in sin did my mother conceive me" (Psalm 51:5).

But the Lord Jesus Christ, our Redeemer, by His atoning
work on the Cross took the sin-scarred and broken vessel,
"man," and by His wisdom and redemptive grace made him
over, as a skillful potter mends a shattered vase. "Therefore if
any man be in Christ, he is a new creature: old things are
passed away; behold, all things are become new" (II Corinthians 5:17). "For we are his workmanship created *in Christ
Jesus . . .*" (Ephesians 2:10).

3. *God Has a Definite Plan for the Life of Every Child
of His Because We Are His New Creation in Christ for the
Purpose of Performing Good Works.* "For we are his work-
manship, created in Christ Jesus *unto good works . . .*"
(Ephesians 2:10). In other words, we are saved to serve.
Saved "by grace . . . through faith . . . not of ourselves . . .
not by works" (Ephesians 2:8-9), but "unto good works"
(Ephesians 2:10). The first cry of the new-born babe in
Christ who desires "the sincere milk of the word" (I Peter
2:1) is "Lord, what wilt thou have me *to do?*" (Acts 9:6).

4. *God Has a Definite Plan for the Life of Every Child*

of His Because He Has Fore-ordained That We Should Walk in These Good Works. "For we are his workmanship, created in Christ Jesus, unto good works, which God *hath before ordained* that we should walk in them" (Ephesians 2:10). Not only are we saved to serve, but God has carefully planned and mapped out this service for us, indeed minutely decreed and appointed it for us, as well as prepared us for it long before we were born.

What a truth is this! God has a plan for every life in Christ Jesus. How it should make our hearts leap with holy anticipation to find and enter into that plan!

II. God's Plan for the Life of Every Child of His Is the Best Possible Plan

Yielding our lives completely to the divine purpose is the prerequisite for receiving the plan. There would be little use of God to reveal His program to us if we were not willing to accept and follow it. Many believers hesitate to yield because they are filled with doubt that God's will is best. They fondly imagine that they can plan their own lives better than God! Nothing, however, could be more unreasonable. Shall not He, the Omniscient One, who made us, who knows our end from our beginning, who is acquainted with our talents and limitations and our thoughts afar off, be better qualified to plan our future, than we who are weak, blundering straying creatures? God's plan is most assuredly the best plan devisable for us.

1. *God's Plan Is the Best Plan for Us Because It Is Adapted to Us Individually.* The apostle not only clearly indicates that God has prepared the plan for us, but what is just as necessary — He has prepared us for the plan. We are "created in Christ Jesus unto good works which God hath before ordained that *we* should walk in them" (Ephesians 2:10). By birth, environment, natural endowments, education, personality and in multitudinous other ways God has prepared us for this service.

Both the plan and those for whom it is planned illustrate the infinite variety of the divine Architect. As He has not made two stars alike, nor two leaves or snowflakes, so He has not created any two people exactly alike. Nor has He made any two plans alike. Each plan is an individual specification for a particular life. The different plans show the same variety as the persons for whom they are planned.

It is a tremendous truth to challenge our yieldedness to God that in all the ages there never has been nor will there ever be another person exactly like you or I. God has constituted us that we alone can reach certain individuals. Our personality given over to Christ and fitted into the divine will is the only medium for their seeing the beauty of Christ. How this fact should grip our hearts and impress upon us the solemn responsibility which is ours to be found in God's plan.

2. *God's Plan Is the Best Plan for Us Because It Brings the Highest Glory to God.* There is no more important consideration in all our decisions, dealings and relationships as Christians than God's glory. "Whether therefore ye eat, or drink, or whatsoever ye do, do all to the glory of God" (I Corinthians 10:31). This must ever be our guiding principle of action in all matters, but especially in that most vital issue of our relationship to God's will and our adjustment to God's plan.

God is glorified when we make known to a lost world the glories of His grace, the wonders of His salvation in Christ, and the blessings of faith in His Word and His will. His plan for each life provides for the maximum degree of usefulness in this holy service. When we find and enter into God's plan we thus glorify Him most. His glory, moreover, means blessing to men and benefit to ourselves. Men are never more helped than by a yielded Spirit-filled believer, who makes Christ known to them. We ourselves are never more blessed than when blessing our fellowman, and thus glorifying God.

III. God's Plan May Be Discerned and Embraced

Although God's plan is best for our lives, bringing the highest glory to God and the greatest blessing to ourselves and to our fellowman, it may be discerned only partially or missed altogether. This solemn fact demands the most careful inquiry concerning the question how we may find and enter into God's plan.

1. *We Must First of All Believe That God Has Such a Plan for Us.* Until we are persuaded of this fact, we shall display little concern to discover the plan for our own lives. But it is not enough to believe that God has such a plan for us. We must believe this plan is better than all our own planning, otherwise we will never adopt it, or having accepted it, remain in it.

2. *We Must Continually Pray.* We must walk carefully and prayerfully that we do not miss God's plan. Such a spiritual boon as walking in the will of God is hotly contested by Satan, is subject to worldly temptations, and is contrary to the cravings of our old nature. Prayer alone, which initially enables us to discern God's plan, will enable us to stay in it, when pressure becomes strong to forsake it.

3. *We Must Yield.* The glorious step of giving ourselves unreservedly and in fullest abandon to the wondrous Saviour who gave Himself so unreservedly for us on Calvary must be lengthened into a life attitude. We must keep on yielding, always on the basis of the original decisive act when we once-for-all gave ourselves to God in solemn dedication. Maintaining this spirit of surrender, we need not be anxious about missing God's plan. Our loving Saviour has a beautiful way of overruling small mistakes when the heart is right and the life yielded.

4. *We Must Wait.* God's plan is not unfolded to us all at once. The divine Architect does not allow us to see the whole blueprint. He shows us the program little by little as we wait upon Him in faith and prayer. If the way ahead is

uncertain, a stop is more important than a step. When the cloud lifts, then we are to journey, as God's people of old — never before.

Consecration, moreover, may not be dislocation. Our eternal Friend with infinite tenderness gives us His own nail-pierced hand, and goes before us to show us the way. Need we fear with such a Companion? Dare we hold back with such a Guide? May we not rest assured that it will be a glorious path all the way? May we not expect to see a "light in the sky, from the palace on high, when we come to the end of the road?"

> God wrested sharply from my hand
> A treasure — plan that I had planned.
> And bade me wait on His command.
>
> He overturned my aims for me
> And left me groping anxiously;
> Bewildered where I could not see.
>
> Then like a blinding sun at night,
> He flashed upon my startled sight
> His plan for guiding me aright.
>
> An untried path, and untried way,
> A hitherto despised essay
> Disclosed His will. Should I obey?
>
> With heart depressed and secret tears,
> I took His hand to face the years;
> Quiescent, but indwelt with fears.
>
> To my complete and frank surprise
> His way led out to shining skies.
> So bright that I must shade my eyes.
>
> A moon-lit path, beset with flowers,
> A rock ofttimes, but gracious hours,
> With love and praise, His suns, His showers.
>
> What if He had not brushed aside
> My aims for me, nor me denied,
> But let me have my will to ride?
>
> —H. S. McRoberts

Putting God First in Our Lives

. . . Make me thereof a little cake first, and bring it unto me, and after make for thee and for thy son (I Kings 17:13).

THE CARDINAL SIN of our day is the widespread practice, even among professing Christian people, of relegating God to a secondary place in life. The Church of Christ is weak and unable to meet the tremendous challenge of the hour because multitudes who name the name of Christ have put God on the periphery rather than in the center of their thinking.

Great numbers of professing believers, many who are doubtlessly truly regenerated children of God, have never given themselves to the Lord, have never accepted God's plan for their lives and are not living a holy life of separation from evil. Caught in the strong currents of a grossly materialistic society, in which people for the most part think in terms of dollars and cents and profit and loss, and where multitudes are either too busy making or spending money, or enjoying the things money can buy to think much about God, many Christians know little of the power and the blessings of complete consecration.

I. PUTTING GOD FIRST INVOLVES UNFALTERING FAITH

Being creatures adapted to residence in a physical realm governed by natural law, in which God and the supernatural sphere of spirit are not knowable through mere sensory perception or human research, it is necessary for everyone who would experience God and His divine power to "walk by faith, not by sight" (II Corinthians 5:7). Because man is what he is, finite, weak, sinful, severely limited as a creature of the natural realm and because God is what He is, the Creator, infinite, omnipotent, unlimited in every sense as the Framer of the spiritual as well as the natural spheres, it is impossible to "please" Him "without faith" (Hebrews 11:6). Any other attitude on man's part in his approach to God dishonors God.

1. *We Must Believe God Is.* "For he that cometh to God must believe that he is . . ." (Hebrews 11:6). Unless we are persuaded God exists, we shall never put Him first in our lives. If we really believe He does exist and *take* Him as the Scriptures reveal Him to be, the Creator of the Universe and man's Redeemer, and do not *make* Him a mere product of our imagination, we shall be bound by all the laws of consistency to give Him first place in our lives. Any other position is utterly illogical and sinful.

The account of Elijah and the widow of Zarephath recounted in I Kings 17 illustrates the importance of faith in dealing with God. It was the widow's faith in the Word of God coming to her through His prophet that brought her the blessing. "Make me thereof a little cake *first*, and bring it unto me, and after make for thee and for thy son" (I Kings 17:13).

This was a staggering request considering the widow's poverty and the dire straits to which she had been reduced by the prolonged famine in Israel. She had meal and oil enough for only one more cake. Should she give this to a complete stranger when it was all that stood between starvation for herself and her son? But she believed God existed. She believed He was what He is and would do what He said He would do through His Word which came to her through His servant. "For thus saith the Lord God of Israel, The barrel of meal shall not waste, neither shall the cruse of oil fail, until the day that the Lord sendeth rain upon the earth" (I Kings 17:14).

2. *We Must Believe God Is a Rewarder of Them Who Diligently Seek Him.* "For he that cometh to God" must not

only believe that "he is" but also that "he is a rewarder of them that diligently seek him" (Hebrews 11:6). This woman had faith to believe God was not asking her to give up one world without offering her another.

It is beautiful to note, too, that God tenderly prepared the poor widow for the severer test by an easier one. As the prophet of God, exhausted from a long journey, saw the woman at eventide gathering a few sticks to prepare the last morsel of food she had for herself and her son, his first request was not for food, but only for water. "Fetch me, I pray thee, a little water in a vessel, that I may drink" (I Kings 17:10). In the protracted drought water was scarce enough, but food was more precious than fine gold when famine stalked through the land like a ravenous beast.

As the widow's faith rose to meet the petition for water, God prepared her for the request for food. "And as she was going to fetch it," the prophet called to her, and said, "Bring me, I pray thee, a morsel of bread in thine hand" (I Kings 17:11). It was then that faith received its supreme test. "Fear not; go and do as thou hast said, but make me thereof a little cake first" (verse 13).

Had this woman failed in the lesser test, she would never have had the opportunity of the greater, nor the inestimable privilege of knowing God, like Abraham, and all God's people of faith, as her "exceeding great reward" (Genesis 15:1).

II. PUTTING GOD FIRST INVOLVES COMPLETE YIELDEDNESS

Faith in the Holy Scripture is a window giving us a clear view into the heart of God. Those who gaze through this window find God to be what the Scriptures testify Him to be, a Being of infinite love and mercy and the Source of all blessings. Those who thus become acquainted with God and see His gracious purposes and provisions for His own, discover that it is a natural and spontaneous course of action to yield themselves to Him in loving surrender and to place Him first in their lives.

1. *Yielding to God Necessitates Continuous Uncompromising Obedience.* This aspect of devotion to God is well illustrated by the widow of Zarephath. When the request came for water we read of no doubt or hesitation on the part of the poor widow, who is a type of the true consecrated steward of God. It was indeed a hard request, and to unbelief, an unreasonable demand. Was not this man, despite the dignity of his appearance, a mere stranger? Why should she take of her meagre supply of water in her dire need and give it away? What was more staggering, why should she part with her last handful of food when starvation was staring her and her son in the face and give it to this chance wayfarer *first?*

Faith does not rationalize or ask questions, however. It obeys simply because God commands. The widow's obedience was thorough because her faith was genuine. We shall never obey God and put Him first in our lives until we believe Him and are willing to yield to Him. Faith is the foundation upon which the superstructure of obedience is erected. We shall only yield as we believe God, and we shall obey only as we keep yielded. It is not difficult in the light of this truth to see why unbelief is the cardinal sin.

2. *Yielding to God Often Requires Willing Sacrifice.* God does not always require the surrender of the nearest and dearest in this life. He sometimes does, however, to test our love. Abraham must be willing to give up his Isaac. Moses must give up a throne. Hannah must surrender her little boy. Jesus must give us His life a ransom for many. The widow must relinquish her last handful of meal and commit her life and that of her son into the hands of Elijah's God.

The supreme sacrifice at Calvary was never made at such tremendous cost to purchase a cheap reprieve from punishment or to furnish an escape from self-denial, or to grant divine indulgence to men to go on living an easy, care-free, selfish existence. We do not enter into the fulness of the meaning of Calvary until the same spirit of sacrifice is repeated in our lives as we yield ourselves completely to God's will.

III. PUTTING GOD FIRST EVENTUATES IN ASSURED GAIN

No one can possibly lose out by putting God first. What at the moment may seem loss turns out sooner or later to be gain. Men are often richest in true wealth when poorest in those things which worldlings reckon as riches. God knows how to enrich us with treasures that are imperishable. He may strip us, but only to clothe us with Himself. He brings us to nothing, only that Christ might be everything.

1. *Putting God First Results in Gain in This Life.* It has its rewards here and now. Who will say this Sidonian widow did not gain by consecrating her little (but her all) to God? Her own supplies were multiplied. Her own needs were met. Her life and that of her son were saved. Her entire future was guarded and blessed by Him Whom she had trusted. Her act of faith lifted her out of oblivion into fame, out of littleness into bigness, and enabled her not only to keep herself from starving, but to keep others alive and thus to perform a great service for God and man. For an entire year she supported one of the greatest of God's prophets, a man who was taken to heaven in a chariot of fire without ever dying.

2. *Putting God First Insures Gain in the Life to Come.* Jesus in His sermon in the synagogue at Nazareth referred to this woman of remarkable faith. "Many widows were in Israel in the days of Elijah . . . but unto none of them was Elijah sent, save unto Sarepta, a city of Sidon, unto a woman that was a widow" (Luke 4:25, 26). God honored her above all the widows in Israel, and gave her the added distinction of special citation by our Lord Himself, because she had faith to put God first.

Her faith will yet be rewarded. "And everyone that

hath forsaken houses, or brethren, or sisters, or father, or mother, or wife, or children, or lands, for my name's sake, shall receive an hundredfold, and shall inherit everlasting life" (Matthew 19:29). No one can be the loser who puts God first. The crass materialism of our age needs to see a living proof of this great truth in the life of every child of God. Then men will begin to see the folly of relegating God to an inferior place or crowding Him out of the life altogether.

All for Jesus, all for Jesus!
    All my being's ransomed powers:
All my thoughts and words and doings,
    All my days and all my hours.

Let my hand perform His bidding,
    Let my feet run in His ways;
Let my eyes see Jesus only,
    Let my lips speak forth His praise.

Oh, what wonder! how amazing!
    Jesus, glorious King of kings,
Deigns to call me His beloved,
    Lets me rest beneath His wings.

All for Jesus! All for Jesus!
    Resting now beneath His wings;
All for Jesus! All for Jesus!
    Resting now beneath His wings.
                                        —*Mary D. James*

Living a Holy Life

And the very God of peace sanctify you wholly; and I pray God your whole spirit and soul and body be preserved blameless unto the coming of our Lord Jesus Christ. Faithful is he that calleth you, who also will do it (I Thessalonians 5:23, 24).

A TRULY CONSECRATED LIFE is a holy life. If we give ourselves to the Lord and by reliance upon the Holy Spirit walk in God's plans, a holy life is bound to be the result (Gal. 5:16). God's purpose for us is always one of holiness, involving our being separated from sin and worldliness, and our being devoted unto Him. "For this is the will of God, even your sanctification" (I Thessalonians 4:3).

Despite its vast practical importance, there are few truths more misunderstood than the Bible doctrine of holiness or sanctification. Frequently this theme is hopelessly confused with the baptism of the Spirit, with a so-called "second blessing" with such imaginary experiences as sinless perfection or the eradication of the old nature. Quite commonly holiness of life is placed on the low plane of self-effort and human struggle, and the true source, nature and meaning of Bible sanctification confused.

I. A HOLY LIFE HAS ITS SOURCE IN GOD

Natural sweetness and outward morality may often be found in unregenerate people, but true holiness can only be produced in those who are in vital relationship to God. It is impossible for the old nature to bring forth fruit unto holiness. Only the Holy Spirit operating through the new nature in the redeemed child of God is capable of producing a holy walk.

1. *Sanctification Is the Work of God Himself.* "And the *very God of peace* sanctify you . . ." (I Thessalonians 5:23). The contrast is between the futile efforts after holiness of which believers so often imagine themselves capable and the almighty power of sanctification exercised by God. It is difficult for many earnest Christians to see that sanctification is a matter of faith and not of works, resting in Christ and not fleshly struggling, perfection in Christ and not self-improvement, a work of God and not an attainment of man.

It is appalling, too, to see many religious and moral (but unsaved) people trying fondly to live a holy life. The utter impossibility of this lies in the fact that the unregenerate do not possess a new nature nor the Holy Spirit (Romans 8:9; I Corinthians 6:19) and are thus shut up to self-effort, which is just as incapable of producing holiness in the saved as in the unsaved.

The difference between an unsaved person, a saved person not living a holy life, and a saved person living a holy life may be illustrated by three rosebushes viewed first in midwinter and then in June. All of them are leafless, thorny and seemingly lifeless in the winter's frosty sunlight. However, two of them, representing believers, possess life. The third representing an unsaved person is dead. It is just as leafless, thorny and lifeless in June as in January. It is incapable of responding to God's sunlight, warm rains and caressing dews. Similarly the unsaved man cannot respond to God's sanctifying power through His Spirit and His Word because, like the lifeless rose bush, he is dead.

Walking by means of the Holy Spirit (Galatians 5:16) according to the cleansing power of the Word (John 15:3), the beauty and fragrance of the Lord Jesus, "the rose of Sharon" (Song of Solomon 2:1), are produced in the child of God, who lives a holy life by walking "worthy of the vocation" wherewith he was called (Ephesians 4:1).

2. *God's Work of Sanctification Is the Gateway to a*

Deeper Peace. It is not without deep significance that the apostle refers to God in His ministry of sanctification as "the very God of peace," or in more usual English, "the God of peace Himself." The reason for this is that the sanctification which He works in the soul not only involves peace with God, which is the possession of every believer, but the very "peace of God which passeth all understanding" and which guards the heart and the mind (Philippians 4:7) of all who permit the Holy Spirit to direct them into a holy life.

3. *Sanctification Is in Three Aspects.* Much of the confusion that exists in the popular mind concerning the Bible doctrine of holiness is due to a widespread failure to recognize that the Christian is the object of a threefold work of sanctification. First he is *positionally* sanctified in Christ "once for all" the moment he is saved. Our Lord Jesus "is made unto us . . . sanctification" (I Corinthians 1:30). "By the which will we are sanctified through the offering of the body of Jesus Christ once for all" (Hebrews 10:10). The apostle addressed all "in Christ" as "saints," and "sanctified" even the Corinthian believers (I Corinthians 1:2; 6:11), although they were far from being such in daily life (I Corinthians 5:1, 2; 6:1, 7, 8).

Secondly, the believer is being *experimentally* sanctified by the power of God through the Word (John 17:17; II Corinthians 3:18; Ephesians 5:25, 26; II Peter 3:18). This phase of the sanctifying work of God for the believer is *progressive* to a large extent, and accordingly stands in clear contrast to *positional* sanctification, which is unchangeable and wrought "once for all." It was this progressive or experimental aspect of sanctification Paul had in mind when he prayed that "the God of peace" would sanctify the Thessalonian believers "wholly" or "through and through," and experimental sanctification, or the actual living of a holy life, depends upon many factors, such as faith, obedience, yieldedness and walking by means of the Spirit.

Thirdly, the believer will be *ultimately* sanctified when the saints are gathered into the Lord's presence. "When he shall appear, we shall be like him" (I John 3:2) and "conformed to the image of the Son" (Romans 8:29). Thus only at the time of glorification will experimental sanctification be perfected in the believer.

II. A HOLY LIFE INVOLVES THE ENTIRE MAN

Holy living is translating our holy position "in Christ" into a holy experience of Christ. Because we are organically united to the Son of God by virtue of the Holy Spirit's work in baptizing us into Christ's body (I Corinthians 12:13) and into Christ Himself (Romans 6:3, 4), God sees us in this holy place, *because He sees us in His beloved Son.* By faith, enabling us to give ourselves to the Lord and by means of the Spirit walking in God's plan for our lives, we are called upon to reckon upon our position and thus convert it into practice.

1. *A Holy Life Is a Blameless Life.* It is God's purpose and the apostle's prayer that believers be so diligent in converting their holy position in Christ into a corresponding holy walk for Christ that they may be preserved from fault or defect. "And I pray God your whole spirit and soul and body be preserved blameless . . ." The apostle expresses a similar conviction to the Corinthian believers: "So that ye come behind in no gift; waiting for the coming of our Lord Jesus Christ; who shall confirm you unto the end, that ye may be blameless in the day of our Lord Jesus Christ" (I Corinthians 1:7, 8).

2. *A Holy Life Involves Spirit, Soul and Body.* The idea of "the God of peace" sanctifying "wholly" is that of leaving no part of us unsanctified. In experimental sanctification God works upon man as a whole — spirit, soul and body. Sanctification preserves all these three divisions entire, and in their due relation to each other.

Man's spirit is the highest part of his nature which is conscious of and holds communion with God and which thus apprehends realities intuitively, that is, without reasoning upon them. In a sanctified spirit all the faculties of consciousness and communion are fully controlled by and given over to God, and are completely open and responsive to Him.

Man's soul is that division of his being which includes the intellect, the affections and the will. In a sanctified soul the intellectual activities embracing perception, memory, imagination and reason are separated from sin and selfishness and dedicated to God. Taste for art, music, literature is likewise altered and directed into Christ-honoring channels. The affections are changed so that Christ is given first place before those nearest and dearest to us in earthly relationships. The will is yielded to God completely so that God's plan may be worked out in the life.

III. A Holy Life Has Its Incentive in God's Faithfulness

Those who look for the dynamic and the encouragement for holy living in themselves and their faithfulness are doomed to failure and disappointment. Since sanctification is God's work in us, the true impulse to holiness is found in looking away from our unfaithfulness to His faithfulness, from our failure to His power, from our weakness to His strength.

1. *God's Character Guarantees Sanctification.* "Faithful is he . . . who also will do it" (I Thessalonians 5:24). The apostle mentions the coming of the Lord and prays not so much that the Thessalonians might be preserved from sin during the interim, but hastens in eager anticipation to the coming itself, and hopes that the Thessalonians will be found to have been preserved *at* the coming. He quickly adds that he will not be disappointed because of God's faithfulness.

The Thessalonians being *positionally* sanctified because "in Christ" will also be *ultimately* sanctified or glorified at the coming of the Lord. "For whom he did foreknow, he also did *predestinate to be conformed to the image of his Son*"

(Romans 8:29). God's faithfulness alone guarantees this glorious destiny of the believer.

2. *God's Call Assures Sanctification.* "Faithful is he who *calleth you,* who also will do it." God would forfeit His character for keeping His promise if He called and did not enable men to obey the call, or to live in a way to honor the call, or to be assured of the final fruition of the call. "Moreover, whom he did predestinate, them he also called: and whom he called, them also he justified: and whom he justified, them he also glorified" (Romans 8:30).

3. *God's Power Produces Sanctification.* "Faithful is he who calleth you, who *also will do it.*" God's power gives us an unchangeable and unforfeitable position as "saints" or "sanctified ones" when we believe on Christ as our Saviour. His power secures every such "saint" glorification or perfect conformity to the "image of his Son." His power is at the disposal of the "saint" to live as a saint during his pilgrimage in a sinful world.

But God can only sanctify a believer experimentally to the degree that the believer is willing to be sanctified. Failure of the believer to allow God to thus sanctify him does not forfeit his position as a saint nor his future conformity to Christ. It does, though, incur God's disciplinary action against the believer, curtailment of the believer's usefulness and loss of reward for unfaithful living and serving, together with forfeiture of the deep joy of fellowship and the peace of God flooding the believer's heart.

Too great a price is this for the Christian to pay to live a careless and selfish life! The rewards for a holy life are incalculable both for time and eternity. Let us, therefore, walk that we too may be blameless in the presence of our Lord Jesus and "not be ashamed before him at his coming" (I John 2:28). Let us live that we may rather "have boldness in the day of judgment" (I John 4:17) and abounding joy and wide usefulness as we serve God in our allotted time.

CHAPTER FIVE

THE PATHWAY OF SERVICE

Mending the Saints

And he gave some apostles; and some, prophets; and some evangelists; and some, pastors and teachers; for the perfecting (mending) of the saints for the work of the ministry (Ephesians 4:11, 12).

All of us are acquainted with the necessity of mending or repairing various articles we use in our daily lives. The refrigerator or the radio goes out of order. We call a mechanic. The car breaks down. We call the garage. A suit or other article of dress is torn. We send it to the tailor. So it is with various items. In course of time they wear out or break down and need mending or repairing. Christians are much the same way. They often break down and need spiritual repairing to enable them to continue in their work of serving.

I. God Has Made Full Provision for Mending His Saints

We are *His* saints. We are called to do *His* work. It is He who worketh in us both to will and to do of His own good pleasure. Shall we not expect Him, who restores the soul, to make adequate provision for keeping us in a state of blessing and usefulness?

1. *God Has Made Full Provision for Mending His Saints by Christ's Gifts to the Individual Believer.* "But unto everyone of us is given grace according to the measure of the gift of Christ" (Ephesians 4:7). It is significant that God first gives everyone of His saints grace. No believer is excluded. It is this marvelous blessing that works in us to mend and restore our spiritual lives. God's grace, moreover, is "ac-

cording to the measure of the *gift* of Christ." He, the bounteous Giver, dispenses it freely according to His own sovereign will and pleasure as it pleases Him and as He discerns the need for it in the lives of His loved ones.

The apostle closely connects God's rich gift of grace with the ascension of Christ. "Wherefore he saith, when he ascended up on high, he led captivity captive, and *gave* gifts unto men" (Ephesians 4:7, 8). It was in His death, resurrection, and return to the Father that Jesus won the superlative victory over sin, death, and hell and "gave gifts unto men." We perhaps do not know all that the word "gifts" implies, but we do know that the Holy Spirit was the great ascension gift. He came to be the skilful Mender of our lives, to make real *in* us what Christ accomplished on the Cross *for* us, and to endow us with various spiritual gifts for service (I Corinthians 12:8-10).

2. *God Has Made Full Provision for Mending His Saints by Christ's Gifts to the Church As a Whole.* The risen, glorified Lord has given certain talented and Spirit-endued men to His body, the Church, to meet the need in each assembly. The Lord in bestowing these gifted men in His infinite wisdom determines the sphere and place of their service. Nothing is left to self-will. It is the Holy Spirit who said to the Church at Antioch, "Separate *Me* Barnabas and Saul for the work whereunto I have called them" (Acts 13:2). It is the Holy Spirit who forbade Paul "to preach the Word in Asia," who suffered him not to go into Bithynia, but who brought him down to Troas, there to receive the vision to go into Macedonia (Acts 16:6-10).

The talented men, Christ's gifts to the Church to be media of blessing and the human instruments through whom the Holy Spirit can mend the saints, are enumerated. "He himself (emphatic) gave some apostles; and some prophets; and some evangelists; and some, pastors and teachers" (Ephesians 4:11). The "apostles," strictly speaking, were confined to the closing of the canon and the establishment of Christianity. Yet in a broader sense men like Polycarp, Augustine, Luther, Wesley, Moody and other unusually endowed and widely-used servants of God may be thought of in a certain sense at least as apostles.

"Prophets" are "forthtellers" rather than "foretellers," yet are men with a keen discernment of the meaning of the prophetic Scriptures, enabling them to interpret the Word of God in the light of the contemporary world situation. "Evangelists" are heralds of God's redeeming grace in Christ, His gifts to the Church at large. Pastors and teachers are His gifts to the local church, whose task is principally to instruct and build up the people of God in the faith. Through His gifts and grace God has amply provided for the mending of His saints.

II. God Has a Precise Purpose for Mending His Saints

He is a God of Purpose. With Him there is no chance or hit-or-miss action. Here as elsewhere God's intention is apparent.

1. *God's Purpose First of All in Mending His Saints Is to Fit Them for the Work of the Ministry.* He gives talented men to the church "in order fully to equip His people for the work of serving" (Weymouth). We are saved to serve, and God counts our service important. He undertakes on our behalf that we may be fully qualified to perform it. The power of God not only works in us to make us useful, but to keep us usable.

2. *God's Purpose in Mending His Saints Moreover, Is That They May Edify the Body of Christ.* It is the divine plan to build up the Church. "Upon this rock I *will build* my church" (Matthew 16:18) are the words of Jesus. However, unless God's people are continually mended by the ministry of the Spirit they soon would become a force for pulling down God's work rather than building it up. Wherever the Spirit is hindered in His ministry of mending the

saints, whether in the believer's heart or through the apostle, prophet, evangelist, pastor, or teacher, the development of God's work is arrested and God's people may become destructive rather than constructive in life and testimony.

3. *God's Purpose in Mending His Saints Is Further That They May Promote Christian Unity and Maturity.* It is the divine plan that all believers "come in the unity of faith and of the knowledge of the Son of God, unto a perfect man, unto the measure of the stature of the fulness of Christ" (Ephesians 4:13). This is true scriptural unity, not on the basis of compromising the foundational truths of Christianity, as in the modern ecumenical movement, but resting securely upon full accurate knowledge of the Son of God, His glorious Person and finished work, and having as its goal spiritual adulthood and full-orbed Christian maturity.

Such Christian growth automatically insures immunity from strictly children's diseases, especially from the malady of *spiritual instability,* which the apostle specifically singles out. "That ye henceforth be no more children, tossed to and fro, and carried about with every wind of doctrine, by the sleight of men, and cunning craftiness, whereby they lie in wait to deceive" (Ephesians 4:14). He changes his metaphor from a stormy ocean with those ensnared by unsound teachings likened to helpless little children adrift upon the raging waves to a gambling den, where the dupes of false isms are compared to innocent youngsters fleeced by wily dishonest gamesters.

4. *Lastly, God's Purpose in Mending His Saints Is That They May Speak the Truth in Love.* It is an impressive contrast. Instead of being ignorant and uncertain of the truth and at the mercy of false teachers, the mature saint, mended and matured by the faithful ministry of God's Spirit, is enabled to "speak the truth in love" (Ephesians 4:15). It is often difficult to speak the truth. It is always more difficult to speak the truth *in love.* There is a subtle temptation to be

harsh and unkind in proclaiming the truth, or unloving and critical in standing for it. Only a fine maturity produced by the indwelling, inworking Holy Spirit in the believer's heart can enable him "to speak the truth in love." God mends His saints with this ability in view that we "may grow up into him in all things, who is the head, even Christ" (Ephesians 4:15).

Is it not a comfort to know that God in His rich mercy has not only gloriously saved us but made every provision for any repairs or adjustments that may be necessary along the way in our Christian life and testimony? His own wonderful grace is ours for the asking. The fulness of His blessed Holy Spirit is ours for the taking. He sends His own servants with the Word of Truth that we may be thoroughly furnished unto all good works and made to stand perfect and complete in all the will of God. Our God has done all to insure us a radiant effective life of service. *He has not failed us.* Dare we fail *Him?*

> A charge to keep I have,
>   A God to glorify,
> A never-dying soul to save,
>   And fit it for the sky.
>
> To serve the present age,
>   My calling to fulfill;
> O may it all my powers engage,
>   To do my Master's will!
>
> Arm me with jealous care,
>   As in Thy sight to live,
> And O Thy servant, Lord, prepare,
>   A strict account to give!
>
> —Charles Wesley

Radiating the Beauty of the Lord

And let the beauty of the Lord our God be upon us . . .
(Psalm 90:17). But we all, with open face beholding as in a
glass the glory of the Lord, are changed into the same image
from glory to glory as by the Spirit of the Lord (II Corinthians
3:18).

There is no more important qualification for effective
Christian service than to live in such a manner that the beauty
of the Lord our God will be produced in us by the Holy Spirit
and become visible through us to those about us. This is God's
purpose in mending our lives for the work of serving, as
well as His intention in all the gracious ministries of His
Spirit operating in us. He has predestinated us "to be conformed to the image of his Son" (Romans 8:29). Even now
He is in the process of reproducing that image in us. He
desires that we may not only be channels of blessing in
eternity. It is His longing as well that we with unveiled
face beholding as in a mirror "the glory of the Lord" shall
be "changed into the same image from glory to glory" (II
Corinthians 3:18) so that in this life we may make Christ
visible to men, thus making possible their being drawn unto
Him.

The divine beauty revealed in Christ becomes visible
to us by faith. He whom we have never seen makes Himself
known as the One "altogether lovely" (Song of Solomon
5:16) and "fairer than the children of men" (Psalm 45:2),
as we accept Him as our Saviour, crown Him as our Lord,
and follow on to know Him of whom Zechariah exclaimed
centuries before His birth in Bethlehem: ". . . How great is

136

his goodness and how great is his beauty!" (Zechariah 9:17).

The divine beauty as revealed in Christ not only becomes visible *to* us, however, but also *through* us. Men see Christ in us when the Holy Spirit has full control of our lives to conform them to the image of God's Son.

I. We Need to Discern and Appreciate the Beauty of the Lord Our God to Serve Him

To know God's grace and beauty as revealed in Christ is to love Him. The better we know Him, the more shall we love Him. The more we love Him, the better shall we be able to serve Him. For this reason the highest possible aim of the believer is that expressed in the immortal words of the the great apostle, which may be characterized as his life's motto —*"that I may know him!"* (Philippians 3:10). No finer goal is possible to a human soul than to reach out in holy desire to become more intimately acquainted with the superlative loveliness of Christ and to explore the boundless outreaches of His unfathomable love and grace. This is indeed to see and appreciate "the beauty of the Lord our God," which the psalmist prayed might be communicated to him. This is indeed to receive the true dynamic for a life of devoted service.

Although "the beauty of the Lord" transcends human thought and language, several things may be said concerning it.

1. *The Beauty of the Lord Our God Is Infinite in Its Magnificence.* Like Himself and all His attributes, God's beauty, which is the ineffably glorious effect of all His characteristics, is infinite. As such it stretches above and beyond finite comprehension. This does not mean that God's grandeur may not be seen and appreciated by His finite creatures. It does suggest, however, that even God's highest creatures, the angels, cannot fully fathom the divine majesty. Only God Himself can fully glimpse the effulgence of His own splendor.

Before "the Lord high and lifted up, even the seraphim

cover their faces and the perpetual anthem is "Holy, holy, holy, is the Lord of hosts: the whole earth is full of his glory" (Isaiah 6:1-3). "The likeness of the glory of the Lord" was so overpoweringly resplendent to Ezekiel (Ezekiel 1:28) and John (Revelation 1:17) that they fell upon their faces as dead men. A mere veiled manifestation of the divine majesty at Bethel made Jacob cry out, "How dreadful is this place! this is none other but the house of God, and this is the gate of heaven" (Genesis 28:17).

2. *The Beauty of the Lord Our God Is Reflected in Creation.* Although we can never completely understand the glory of the Maker, His beauty everywhere radiates from that which He has made. Yet creation is only a feeble reflection of the splendor of the Creator, as the earthen vessel only dimly indicates the power and the skill of the potter who fashioned it.

Since creation, even though marred by sin, is so grandly magnificent, *what must the magnificence of the Creator be?* The human eye can only wander among the starry heavens at night and exclaim with the psalmist, "O Lord, our Lord, how excellent is thy name in all the earth! who hast set thy glory above the heavens . . . When I consider the heavens, the work of thy fingers, the moon and stars which thou hast ordained: what is man that thou art mindful of him? or the son of man that thou visitest him?" (Psalm 8:1-4).

Or the human vision can glimpse the splendors of the skies by day and repeat with the ancient poet: "The heavens declare the glory of God: and the firmament showeth knowledge. There is no speech nor language, where their voice is not heard. Their line is gone out through all the earth, and their words to the end of the world. In them he hath set a tabernacle for the sun, which is as a bridegroom coming out of his chamber, and rejoiceth as a strong man to run a race" (Psalm 19:1-5).

3. *The Beauty of the Lord Our God Is Featured in*

Redemption. Creation's witness to the glory of the Creator is eloquent, but for the most part silent. Of course, there is the thundering roar of the cataract—the restless surge of the sea —the moan of the wind in the forest. But the stars speak silently. The sun and moon utter no words. The leafy tree is a mute witness to God's loveliness.

But when the Eternal Word "was made flesh" and "dwelt among us" God's glory became marvelously visible. God's Word became intimately vocal. God's beauty became humanly understandable in Jesus of Nazareth. "And we beheld his *glory,* the glory as of the only begotten of the Father, *full of grace and truth*" (John 1:14).

Creation has spoken, but not in human words proceeding from human lips. Sunrise and sunset, stars and planets, waterfalls and mountains could never tell forth the heart of God as Jesus tells it forth—by His sinless life, His vicarious atoning death, and His glorious resurrection. The beauty of the divine nature is revealed through the medium of His perfect human nature. God's inmost heart of love, compassion, and grace is laid bare for man's need and man's salvation in the Lord Jesus Christ.

When we behold Him our eyes "see the King in his beauty" (Isaiah 33:17). To us who believe in Him now He is "a crown of glory," and "a diadem of beauty," as He will be to repentant Israel at His second advent (Isaiah 28:5). To us who follow Him now He is "the branch of the Lord . . . beautiful and glorious" (Isaiah 4:2). We say with the psalmist, "Honor and majesty are before him: strength and beauty are in his sanctuary" (Psalm 96:6). Like "Isaiah, when he saw his glory" (John 12:41) and heard Him say: "Whom shall I send, and who will go for us?" (Isaiah 6:8), our glad response becomes, "Here am I, send me."

II. We Need to Desire and Appropriate the Beauty of the Lord Our God to Live for Him

As fallen creatures, who have accepted God's redemption in Christ, we are to show forth God's glory, not only by our service, but by our lives. Fallen men, who have not received Christ's salvation, cannot glorify Him, either in life or service. On the other hand, all God's *unfallen* creatures reflect His glory and beauty. Man as He came from the Creator's hand was made in the image and likeness of God (Genesis 1:26). Unfallen man, clothed with God's light and glory, did not know the shame and nakedness of sin. It was only after the fall that the divine image in man was marred and man became ungodly, wicked and destitute of the "beauty of holiness."

It was to regenerate and restore fallen man that Jesus came to die on the Cross, bearing our sins in His own body on the tree. Man ruined and made ugly by sin desperately needs to be transformed into the likeness and image of God which he lost.

1. *The Beauty of the Lord Our God Is Wonderfully Transformative.* To those who come to Christ — no matter how buffeted by Satan or completely distorted from the divine image—God gives the "beauties of holiness" (Psalm 110:3) for the "ashes" of sin (Isaiah 61:3). "If any man be in Christ, he is a new creation: old things are passed away; behold, all things are become new (II Corinthians 5:17). The miracle of regeneration restores the soul to the divine image.

No change is quite so thoroughgoing as the touch of God upon the soul in conversion. The hand of the master Potter can remake the vessel shattered by sin into a product far more beautiful than the old. The infinite Musician can re-tune the discordant life and bring forth exquisite harmonies. When the meaning of the sinless life and the vicarious death of Christ dawns upon the soul, the beauty of God's holiness floods it as the rays of the rising sun chase away the darkness of the night.

2. *The Beauty of the Lord Our God Is Humanly Visible.* In our Lord Jesus God's infinite glory became finite and humanly comprehensible. He who sees the Son sees the Father also (John 14:9). All the glory of God radiates from the Son and in a manner men may see and appropriate. To understand Jesus is to discover the wondrous beauty of God's heart.

To those who know Him as Saviour and Lord, Jesus is "the rose of Sharon and the lily of the valleys" (Song of Solomon 2:1). In meditating upon the beauty of Christ the ancient bard envisioned a scene of transcendent loveliness. He saw the fertile plain of Sharon, extending from Joppa to Carmel, carpeted with gorgeous wild flowers, doubtless the wild tulip or the anemone, the exquisite red variety of the latter being a marked feature of the valleys of Palestine in springtime, especially in the plain of Sharon. Or perchance the poet refers to the white sweet-scented narcissus common in the springtime in Palestinian fields.

The lily was so much at home in Palestinian dells that it was styled "the lily of the valley." It was a lovely sweet-scented bloom dropping a myrrh-like perfume (Song of Solomon 5:13). Whatever plants are meant, the figures present the superlative excellence and loveliness of Christ, who is "altogether lovely" (Song of Solomon 5:16).

This altogether lovely One, manifested in and through our lives by the Holy Spirit, refines our hearts and enables us to glorify God by our thoughts, words and actions. A life thus refined makes possible God-honoring service. Ministry for God not backed up by a life lived for God is mockery. But a life filled with the fragrance of Christ and manifesting the beauty of the Lord brings the invisible God into visible contact with men in their sin and in their need.

Wherever and whenever a life hid with Christ in God

moves among men, it is as though Jesus of Nazareth once more walks among us, now no longer confined to the hills and dales of Palestine, but treading the highways and byways of the earth, making Himself visible in and through His people, His earthly Body, of which He is Head (Ephesians 1:22-23). Wherever there are sin and sorrow, wherever there are broken hearts and broken homes, wherever there are captives of sin and slaves of Satan, once more in the person of His redeemed children we see Jesus of Nazareth anointed with the Holy Spirit and power and going about "doing good," healing all that are "oppressed of the devil" (Acts 10:38).

III. WE NEED TO DELIGHT IN AND REFLECT THE BEAUTY OF THE LORD TO SERVE OTHERS

It is impossible to live for our Lord and serve Him without living for and serving others. Love for God is the higher exercise and always comprehends love for our fellow man. If we truly love God with all our hearts, we shall love our neighbor as ourselves and serve him in the spirit of Christ.

1. *The Beauty of the Lord Our God Is Marvelously Communicable to Us.* To those who delight to enter the divine court, to "see the King in his beauty," and gaze upon His transcendent loveliness, the divine beauty is imparted. Moses, lingering in God's presence chamber, "wist not that the skin of his face shone" (Exodus 34:29). Like him, all who "behold the glory of the Lord" manifested in Christ "are changed into the same image from glory to glory . . . by the Spirit of the Lord" (II Corinthians 3:18).

It was because David delighted in the Lord that he prayed for the communication of the divine touch upon his soul and life. "Let the beauty of the Lord our God be upon us" (Psalm 90:17) was not only the sweet singer of Israel's earnest petition, but is the heart-cry of every child of God who loves the Lord Jesus in sincerity and truth. The request on behalf of ourselves is a noble one for it expresses the innermost longing of the redeemed heart for God, and the impartation of the divine beauty to our poor lives means the highest delight to the soul.

2. *The Beauty of the Lord Our God Is Marvelously Communicable Through Us to Others.* The prayer for the divine beauty to rest upon the believer himself can scarcely be selfish because it is impossible for him to be blessed in his own life without blessing others. The divine beauty is as marvelously communicable to us as through us. The love of God, which is such a vital part of the divine beauty, is a love that extends to every one in the world. "For God so loved the world that he gave his only begotten son . . ." (John 3:16). The beauty of the Lord coming into the human soul draws it out not only in adoration and worship of God, but in delight and devoted service for men. It puts the woe of the sinner's condition in our hearts, and causes us to go to seek them out, making us willing to spend and be spent for their salvation.

Let the prayer, then, that the beauty of the Lord our God may be upon us be for *ourselves,* that we may find our full delight in God. Let it also be for *others* because in the manifestation of His beauty in us He becomes visible to those around us. And when men behold Him in His attractive power and beauty in His people, it is impossible for them to be the same.

"And I, if I be lifted up from the earth, will draw all men unto me" (John 12:32). He was lifted upon the Cross in shame and agony to die for the sins of a ruined race. He was lifted up from the tomb in resurrection power and exalted far above all principalities and powers at God's right hand as our Priest and Intercessor. If He is meanwhile lifted up in our lives so that He may be seen in His grace and beauty, He will draw all men to Him. There is no attractive power in all the universe like the all-lovely Son of God. Let us lift Him up that men may see Him!

Let the beauty of Jesus be seen in me,
All His wonderful passion and purity;
O Thou Spirit divine,
All my nature refine,
Till the beauty of Jesus be seen in me.

—*Albert Osborn*

Serving With the Fragrance of Love

Then took Mary a pound of ointment, very costly, and anointed the feet of Jesus, and wiped his feet with her hair: and the house was filled with the odor of the ointment (John 12:3). . . . *Thy name is as ointment poured forth, therefore do the virgins love thee* (Song of Soloman 1:3).

The highest and holiest service is that which springs spontaneously from a heart of love for Christ. As song is natural to a lark and beauty to a flower, love ought to be the incentive in all our service for God. It is the one thing supremely necessary and that which gives our service fragrance and acceptance with Him. For this reason as believers in our Lord Jesus Christ we should desire a deeper love for Him.

> More love to Thee, O Christ
> More love to Thee!
> Hear Thou the prayer I make
> On bended knee:
> This is my earnest plea,
> More love, O Christ, to Thee,
> More love to Thee,
> More love to Thee!

Our heart yearning should always be that of the bride in the Song of Solomon: "Let him kiss me with the kisses of his mouth, for thy love is better than wine" (1:2). Wine is symbolical of all earthly and merely natural joys. When the incomparable preciousness of His love is realized, and when it is esteemed of more value than all the joys of this life, then its manifestation will be given and its full preciousness realized.

This is the secret of the love for Christ which is found in "virgin" hearts, or hearts uncorrupted by worldly influences and attachments. "Because of the fragrance of thy good ointments thy name is as ointment poured forth, therefore do the virgins love thee" (Song of Solomon 1:3). Such virgin hearts alone can fully appreciate the "fragrance" of Christ's "good ointments," and see the beauty and agreeableness of His Holy Spirit working in them, producing the gifts and graces of the Christian life and acceptable service. Such virgin hearts alone can know His name "as ointment poured forth."

When Jesus appeared from the bosom of the Father upon earth and God had visited to redeem His people, the ointment was poured forth. Its fragrance was wafted abroad. Lovers were attracted by it. His ointments savored sweetly to the distraught widow of Nain, whose son Jesus raised from the dead. The poor distracted Syrophoenician woman perceived the fragrance of His ministry and applied to Him on behalf of her desperate need. Mary of Bethany likewise scented the fragrance of Him who is "the lily of the valleys" and "the rose of Sharon." When He came to the little home in Bethany, amidst the busy preparation to welcome Him, she sensed (perhaps only vaguely), but she *sensed* nevertheless, that never again would *such* a visitor cross their humble threshold—not even if the Emperor in all his pomp should journey from Rome to pay them a visit. His name became to her awakened spirit "like ointment poured forth." She saw Him as the Son of God come from the bosom of the Father to die for the sins of a ruined race. She saw Him crucified, risen, exalted and coming again as "King of kings and Lord of lords."

"Then took Mary a pound of ointment of spikenard, very costly, and anointed the feet of Jesus, and wiped his feet with her hair: *and the house was filled with the odor of the ointment*" (John 12:3). Why was this ointment so sweet?

Why haven't almost two thousand years reduced its fragrance? Why have countless faithful souls scented its rare aroma? Why have the passing centuries been perfumed with its rare odor?

Was it because it was pure nard, a redolent oil extracted from the roots of a scarce plant, and afforded only by the wealthy to anoint themselves? Was the exquisite odor or its great costliness (mentioned by Pliny) the reason why its use here in connection with the Saviour's visit to the little home in Bethany has perpetuated its fame? Nay, far more lavish gifts of perfume have been forgotten in the ceaseless march of the centuries. But this display will never be forgotten. It will live on to bless the world. Why? Because it was the *sincere and genuine expression of deep love and devotion to the Lord Jesus expressed in service.* If His love to us is incomparably precious to us who have virgin hearts, so also is our love for Him much more precious to Him Whose great heart is pained by the first manifestation of our leaving our "first love" (Revelation 2:4).

I. THE OINTMENT WAS THE EXPRESSION OF A GENEROUS LOVE

1. *It Was Love That Lavishly Gave Its Best.* There is little doubt that Jesus had a special love for this family in Bethany. There is little doubt that they had a special love for Him. We can be sure that they took particular pains to make this last visit of the Saviour to their home a token of their deep gratitude to Him for raising Lazarus from the dead. If ever their quiet house nestled among the trees and flowers was in festive mood, it was on this occasion. If ever they brought out the best, it was now. We are given a momentary glance only into their entertainment. "They made him a supper." It was the finest supper that ever graced the little home. That is certain. Nothing was too good. The

finest they could possibly have must be had today! He who had done so much for them must have their best.

"Martha served." Here was a ceaselessly restless love that must express itself in action. How eager she was that He who had called her brother from the tomb after he had been dead four days, should have the best. "But Lazarus was one of them that sat at the table with him." He could most honor the Saviour by being with Him at the table as a monument and proof of the great miracle Christ had wrought. Martha could most honor Him by serving, so *she served*. Lazarus could most honor Him by sitting at table with Him, so *he sat at table*.

There was a deeper, more spiritual love in that little family which must express itself and leave its fragrant touch to immortalize the occasion. "Then Mary took a pound of ointment of spikenard, very costly . . . and anointed the feet of Jesus." She could honor the Master most by anointing His feet with the precious ointment, so *she anointed His feet*. It was a lavish gift, and to hearts not fired by spiritual love and insight, an extravagant waste. It was like throwing a half hundred dollars away in days when poverty abounded, and money could buy much more than now.

But love sought the best it had and lavishly poured it out. Mary doubtless had the precious ointment laid away to use sparingly over a long period. But the sickness, death and resurrection of her brother had deepened the spiritual love that had always filled her heart (Luke 10:30) and the severe test had been a blessing in disguise, weaning her away from such vanities and making her keenly desirous of giving her best to Him who had done so much for her and her family.

2. *It Was Love That Yearned to Express Itself Unstintedly*. So far from sparing necessary charges in His service, Mary is eager to create an occasion of expense in re-

ligion, as the heart that lacks love to Christ is solicitous to avoid it. If she has anything more valuable or costly with which she may honor Christ, that must be brought. He who delivered from death and the grave must have the best. She was like the noble Macedonian Christians, whom the apostle said "first gave their own selves to the Lord" (II Corinthians 8:3). This gift of self made possible Mary's gift. Love was the perfume in the ointment that made it so acceptable as well as generous.

II. THE OINTMENT WAS THE EXPRESSION OF CONDESCEND-ING LOVE

1. *It Was Love That Found Fullest Expression At Jesus' Feet.* Mary not only bestowed her rare ointment upon Christ, but with her own hands lovingly poured its costly contents upon Him. Being a woman of some position, she might have at least ordered one of her servants to do this. What is even more amazing, she did not as usual anoint His head, but His feet. To crown her condescending love "she wiped his feet with her hair." Then, when she was in this humble posture, it was that "the house was filled with the odor of the ointment."

True love, like ointment poured forth, is sweetest when it is most humble. There is no place so secure or so blessed as a position of lowliness in our Lord's presence, humbly bowing at His blessed feet in worship and service. We cannot fall far when we keep low at His feet in adoration and submissive ministry. Moreover, this is not the first time we see true love for Christ finding its rest and joy at His feet. On a former visit we find that Mary "sat at Jesus' feet and heard his word" (Luke 10:39).

2. *It Was Love That Completely Transcended Self.* She did not let a selfish fear of criticism hinder her from the service love dictated. Doubtless the unspiritually minded said she was undignified, over-emotional and extravagant. But

against all the cavils of false modesty or pride, love *won*. Remembering what Christ had done for her and her family, she considered no gesture of gratitude and appreciation beneath her dignity — not even prostrating herself before Him to anoint His feet, and wiping them with the hair of her head.

Was this humble service ignored by the Saviour? Nay, in the act of love rendered to Him she erected to herself an imperishable monument, as lasting as the Gospel, the eternal Word of God. "Verily, I say unto you, Wheresoever this gospel shall be preached in the whole world, there shall also this, that this woman hath done, be told for a memorial of her" (Matthew 26:13; Mark 14:9). Will our gracious God take any less note of the humble acts of love and devotion of other of His own who are in the world?

III. The Ointment Was the Expression of Believing Love

1. *It Was Love That Had Keen Vision.* There was a glowing living faith behind this love that enabled it to see the invisible. There was faith in this love to see that the guest that day was a priest, yea, our Great High Priest, and therefore He was to be anointed as Aaron was! There was faith in this love to see that a king was being entertained that day, yea, the King of kings, and the Lord of lords, and therefore He was to be anointed as David was!

O the glory of faith and the miserable wretchedness of unbelief! Faith opens heaven. Unbelief closes it. Faith brings contact with God. Unbelief cuts it off! Faith brings God's wisdom into our hearts. Unbelief abandons us to our own inventions, and to the folly of our own blindness and sin! Faith pours out the costly ointment in profusion upon the feet of the Saviour. Unbelief begrudges the fragrant oil to anoint the head or the feet even of the Lord of glory, and with selfish voice cries out with mock piety, "Why was not this ointment sold for three hundred denarii and given to the poor?"

Faith touches God and spends itself in grateful service. Unbelief parades with empty religious show and has a form of godliness, but denies the power. It begrudges any gifts of sacrifice to the Saviour. It looks out for self. It fosters the spirit of greed. It would shut up the fragrance of Christ's salvation, and stifle soul-winning and missionary work. It cries with the murderer, Cain, "Am I my brother's keeper?" It would keep back the pouring forth of the spikenard, very costly, at Jesus' feet.

2. *It Was Love That Produced Action.* It was no dreamy, visionary, fruitless pietism, so heavenly that it was not of any earthly good. It was the result of "faith which worketh by love" (Galatians 5:6). Faith which worketh by love accepts God's Anointed and says, "He shall be *my* Anointed." Faith which worketh by love is keen to see that God has poured out upon Christ "the oil of gladness above his fellows" and says, "I will pour out upon Him my best affections above all competitors. He is *my* Lord, I will worship Him." Faith which worketh by love takes the "pound of ointment of spikenard, very costly," and anoints the feet of Jesus, and wipes His feet with her hair! Thus the house, and the whole world, is filled with the odor of the ointment.

Faith which worketh by love lays its treasures of life and possessions at the feet of the Master, and says, "Here am I, send me!" Faith which worketh by love carries the blessed story of redeeming love to the uttermost parts of the earth. It is this fervent, Spirit-born love that delights the heart of the Saviour. It is this pure flame in the heart of Mary that gave the exquisite fragrance to the ointment she poured out long ago in Bethany. It will give the same exquisite fragrance to all our sacrifice and service for Him. May we see it is "the one thing needful," which was not taken away from Mary, and shall not be taken away from us (Luke 10:42).

Jesus, Thine all victorious love
  Shed in my heart abroad:
Then shall my feet no longer rove,
  Rooted and fixed in God.

Refining fire, go through my heart;
  Illuminate my soul;
Scatter Thy life through ev'ry part,
  And sanctify the whole.

No longer then my heart shall mourn,
  While purified by grace,
I only for His glory burn,
  And always see His face.

My steadfast soul, from falling free,
  Shall then no longer move,
While Christ is all the world to me,
  And all my heart is love.
        —Charles Wesley

Shining As Stars

And they that be wise shall shine as the brightness of the firmament; and they that turn many unto righteousness as the stars forever and ever (Daniel 12:3). . . . *In the midst of a crooked and perverse nation, among whom ye shine as lights in the world* (Philippians 2:15).

All of us have had the experience at one time or another of going out into the countryside, away from the glare and glitter of the city, out under God's heaven, and there in silent prayer and meditation, I beheld the stars. How brilliant and sparkling they are as their undimmed splendor shines out in the darkness of the surrounding night. The deepening shade of advancing evening serves only to increase their brilliance and lustre.

God's Word compares true saints to stars. Washed in the blood of the Lamb, serving their blessed Redeemer, beautiful in the light of His love and holiness, God's people rise star-like on the night of surrounding sin. They shine as lights, as lustrous luminaries, in the midst of that "crooked and perverse generation" of which the apostle speaks in the epistle to the Philippians. When the night grows blacker and the darkness becomes more impenetrable as the age hastens on to its end, the lustre of their light is not dimmed, but rather intensified and increased as they serve their Lord who is "the light of the world" (John 8:12).

Unfortunately, however, it is only too true that all Christians are not star-like Christians. It is lamentable that many do not radiate the light of the smallest and feeblest of the heavenly bodies. Their radiance may be more accurately compared to candle light, or the fitful glow of the firefly, or perchance to the last faint glimmer of a dying ember. To be sure there was once a spasmodic burst of joy and radiance when Jesus first came into the life and testimony and service were spontaneous and delightful. The gloom of sin was dissipated. But the winds of doubt and the impure suffocating air of worldliness were allowed to enter. The splendor and joy of salvation began to flicker, grow dim, and well-nigh expire. This ought not to be so! It is a tragic condition God never intended for any of His own. We ought all of us to serve faithfully and to shine for Jesus gloriously. It is our duty! Our high and holy privilege!

Because many fail at this point, the question "How may we become bright star-like Christians?" is of great importance. Where shall we find an answer? The apostle in the second chapter of Philippians gives us the answer. Three injunctions are there presented, which if followed, will enable us to become bright star-like Christians.

I. SHINING AS STARS REQUIRES THAT WE WORK OUT OUR INWROUGHT SALVATION DILIGENTLY

"Work out your own salvation with fear and trembling" (Philippians 2:12). The command is definite. The obligation is inescapable. *"Work out your own salvation!"* But you say, "That is difficult to grasp. Is not salvation by grace alone through faith?" We reply, "Yes, entirely so" (Ephesians 2:8). "Is it not wholly apart from works?" And again we reply, "Most certainly!" "Can salvation be forfeited because of failure to work it out properly?" Our answer again, based upon the Word of God (Romans 8:28-39) is "No!" You ask, "Of what then is the apostle speaking in these verses?" It is clear that he is *not* speaking of working for salvation, but of working it *out!* And what a difference!

1. *Salvation Is Inwrought in Our Hearts by God.*

"Salvation is of the Lord" (Jonah 2:9). A little girl attended church with her mother and listened to a learned divine belabor this text with a legalistic interpretation, insisting that one cannot be saved by grace alone. After the sermon she looked up into her mother's face and said with keen discernment which children often display, "Mother, how can you work it out if you haven't already got it worked in?"

That's the point! It must first be *divinely* worked in before ever it can be *humanly* worked out! Faith in the Lord Jesus is the seed, the invisible root of our spiritual experience concealed within the soul. A holy life and deeds of love and mercy are the glorious outgrowth with stalwart trunk, spreading branches, and luxuriant foliage spreading skyward.

2. *Salvation Is to Be Worked Out by the Believer.* It is immensely important that we understand our salvation as believers and comprehend our wonderful *position* in Christ. This is basic, but it is *not enough.* We must act upon our glorious *position* (Romans 6:3, 4) of union with the Son of God, in death, burial, resurrection (Galatians 2:20) and by *faith* translate our position into everyday *experience* (Romans 6:11). This is working out our inwrought salvation.

Too many believers fail to do this very thing. They are like the little girl who fell out of bed during the night, and when asked the next morning by her mother why she fell out, replied simply, "I don't know, mother, why I fell out, except that I guess I stayed *too near where I got in.*" If we are going to shine for Christ and have a star-like testimony in this scene of darkness and sin, we cannot remain stationary. We must "go on to perfection (maturity)" (Heb. 6:1).

II. SHINING AS STARS REQUIRES THAT WE SERVE OUR LORD JOYFULLY AND SPONTANEOUSLY

"Do all things without murmurings and disputings" (Philippians 2:14). The tendency to mar our service for the Lord by murmuring, complaining and criticizing has always been a common and serious sin among God's people. It was so among God's ancient people Israel. It is so among God's people today. Israel redeemed out of Egypt murmured against Moses. They criticized their diet, although God fed them angel's food. They complained of thirst, although God brought water out of the rock. They found fault with "the way," although it was God's way, and God graciously led them in it with a pillar of cloud by day and a pillar of fire by night.

1. *Joyous and Spontaneous Service Brings Glory to God.* Despite the warning issued to us on the basis of the failure of God's ancient people (I Corinthians 10:10), discontent and dissatisfaction with God's will and God's way are widespread among Christians today and is a serious detriment in many quarters to the progress of God's work. A little poem, entitled "The Critic" contains a parable applicable to many professing believers.

> A little seed lay in the ground
> And soon began to sprout,
> "Now, which of all the flowers around,"
> It mused, "shall I come out?"

Then the little seed bethought itself and said: "I don't want to be a sunflower, for the sunflower is too tall and ungainly, and has no grace or charm. Neither do I want to become a rose, for the rose is rather loud in color, has thorny stems, wilts quickly, and isn't at all practical. And I certainly don't want to be a violet, for the violet is too small, too uncolorful, grows too near the ground in such secluded spots."

The little seed is like some people we all know. It was critical! Critical of everything and everyone around it! It found fault with all its neighbors. Some were too tall, others were too short. Some were too loud in color, others too dull. It had nothing constructive to offer. Its theme was criticism.

> And so it criticized each flower,
> This supercilious seed,
> Until it woke one summer hour
> And found itself *a weed!*

Nothing so bedims our Christian testimony and dishonors God as the spirit of captious criticism. Nothing will more quickly keep us from becoming bright star-like Christians. "Do all things without murmurings and disputings," says the apostle, "that ye may be blameless and harmless, the sons of God, without rebuke, in the midst of a crooked and perverse nation, among whom ye shine as lights (luminaries) in the world" (Philippians 2:14, 15). God's name and cause are blasphemed when His people bring reproach upon Him by murmuring and discord.

2. *Joyous and Spontaneous Service Assures Effective Ministry on Behalf of Men.* "That ye may *become* blameless and harmless." Deftly the apostle suggests they were not all they should have been. As he does so with courtesy and discretion, at the same time he indicates the purpose of avoiding criticism and murmuring. He wants them irreproachable in life and unhindered in service and testimony. Their witness is to be given "in the midst of the crooked and perverse generation." It is not to be in selfish or timorous isolation. They are not to flee away from the world like a monk betaking himself to a cave in the mountains. They are rather to be in the world, but not of the world — in visible contact and attractive power, but separate from its evil.

The necessity for separation from the world is indicated in the apostolic description of it as "a crooked and perverse generation." There could possibly be no more accurate characterization of the unconverted outside world, twisted and distorted by sin, perverted from the way of righteousness and truth. In the midst of this darkness Paul says God's saints are to shine or appear "as lights in the world." He is thinking of the black nocturnal skies studded with multitudinous stars shedding their radiant gleam into the blackness of the night.

Light is needed in the darkness. A candle is of little use in the full glare of the midday sun. As light-bearers and light-reflectors God puts us where we are needed — in dark places. Whether in pagan darkness in Africa or Asia or in the midst of the moral and spiritual darkness of America, God makes no mistakes in placing His witnesses.

He who said, "I am the Light of the world" (John 8:12), who is "the Sun of Righteousness" (Malachi 4:2), and the "bright and morning Star" (Revelation 22:16) can make His servants reflect His glory and in that sense repeat Himself. He also said, "Ye are the light of the world. A city that is set on a hill cannot be hid. Neither do men light a candle, and put it under a bushel, but on a candle stick; and it giveth light unto all that are in the house. Let your light so shine before men, that they may see your good works, and glorify your Father which is in heaven" (Matthew 5:14-16).

The vision of the glorified Son of Man in Revelation presents us with a beautiful picture of God's light-bearing servants. John sees the Lord Jesus walking in the midst of the seven golden candlesticks. His hair is as white as snow, His eyes are like flames of fire, His feet are like polished brass, and His voice is like the sound of many waters. One of the most arresting circumstances in the vision is the fact that the glorious Saviour "had in his right hand seven stars" (Revelation 1:16). The stars are said to be "the angels or ministers of the seven churches" and the seven candlesticks are the "seven churches" (verse 20).

Christ's ministers, then, are like stars. They possess light because they possess Christ. They radiate light because they are placed in dark places to shine. They are held in the right hand of the Son of God Himself. If they are faithful, no one can harm them. If they are unfaithful, they cannot escape. Their position in the right hand of Christ is an exalted and a blessed one. Their prerogative to shine for their Lord and Redeemer is a high and holy one.

Candlesticks (light bearers) and stars belong to the night. We are living in the night of this dispensation. Our business is to shine for Him who has saved us. Our task is to give the light of the Gospel to those who walk "in darkness" and "dwell in the land of the shadow of death" (Isaiah 9:2). It is significant that it is in connection with witnessing that the Apostle Paul gives his final suggestion for becoming bright star-like Christians.

III. SHINING AS STARS REQUIRES THAT WE WITNESS FOR OUR LORD FAITHFULLY

"In the midst of a crooked and perverse generation, among whom ye shine as lights in the world; *holding forth the word of life*" (Philippians 2:15, 16). Taking the Gospel to those who know it not is the unfailing way for Christians to rise star-like on the night of surrounding sin. A soul-winning program, whether for the local church or the individual believer, is a sure remedy against spiritual unhealthiness, manifested in selfish quarrels, criticisms, divisions, carnality and worldliness. The surest way to be delivered from the frustration of self-occupation and to become occupied with Christ is by presenting the Gospel to sinners.

1. *Faithful Witnessing Is Holding Forth the Word of Life.* This glorious message must be given forth because "the god of this world hath blinded the minds of them which believe not, lest the light of the glorious gospel of Christ . . . should shine unto them" (II Corinthians 4:4). As we busy ourselves with "holding forth the word of life," we shall shine as the stars of heaven. "And they that are wise shall shine as the brightness of the firmament; and they that turn many unto righteousness *as the stars* forever and ever" (Daniel 12:3). And who are "the wise?" "He that winneth souls is wise" (Proverbs 11:30). We who were "sometimes

darkness," but now are "light in the Lord" (Ephesians 5:8) can best "walk as children of light" by "holding forth the word of life."

2. *The Word of Life Is a Torch Shining in a Dark Place.* As we hold high the gospel message, it not only sheds light upon the unsaved groping in the night of sin, but at the same time floods our own pathway with radiance. That which is held aloft in our own hand is an instrument of salvation to others and becomes a means of untold blessing to ourselves. "Thy word is a lamp unto my feet and a light to my path" (Psalm 119:105).

Because we lift up the lamp so that others may see, we see better ourselves. More clearly are we able to discern the pitfalls and the dangerous precipices ahead. We find ourselves spared a thousand ills and perils because we are giving forth the Word of Life to others. And to cheer our hearts we see wayfarers and wanderers finding the path of life which we have found, as the Word of Life sheds light upon them. We see tempest-tossed mariners finding the harbor of salvation because of the lights which are kept shining along the shore.

> Dark the night of sin has settled
> Loud the angry billows roar,
> Eager eyes are watching, longing,
> For the lights along the shore.
>
> Trim your feeble lamp, my brother;
> Some poor sailor tempest-tossed,
> Trying now to make the harbor
> In the darkness may be lost.
>
> Let the lower lights be burning
> Send a gleam across the wave!
> Some poor fainting struggling seaman,
> You may rescue, you may save.
> —*Philip P. Bliss*

17358